# THE SHIFTING OF THE
# CORPORATION INCOME TAX

*An Empirical Study of its*
*Short-Run Effect upon the Rate of Return*

# THE SHIFTING OF
# THE CORPORATION
# INCOME TAX

AN EMPIRICAL STUDY OF ITS SHORT-RUN EFFECT
UPON THE RATE OF RETURN

*by*
MARIAN KRZYZANIAK
*and*
RICHARD A. MUSGRAVE

THE JOHNS HOPKINS PRESS
BALTIMORE

Printed in the United States of America

Library of Congress Catalog No. 63–19555

This book has been brought to publication
with the assistance of a grant from
The Ford Foundation.

PREFACE

THE INCIDENCE OF the corporation income tax has been a much discussed problem, and views thereon are implicit in many arguments about tax policy, including the equity of the tax structure, tax effects on growth and so forth. Diverse conclusions have been drawn from the observation of general data, and some of these have shaken the traditional proposition of no short-run shifting. Such conclusions, however, are of limited value. They do not isolate the effects of changes in tax rates, changes which are prone to occur precisely in periods when many other factors in the economy change as well. This study is a first systematic attempt to isolate the tax effect.

To begin with, one must decide just which consequence of the corporation tax rate is to be measured. Is it the effect on prices, wages, factor shares, income distribution by size brackets, the rate of return on capital, the level of investment, excess burdens, or capital movements between sectors of industry? And is one to measure the short- or long-run consequences of the tax? Our choice has been to focus on taxation effects on the rate of return, and to measure those effects which come about rapidly and may be observed in the short run. Our results, therefore, give by no means the entire picture, but they should provide a basis for the exploration of other aspects.

Our first task was to estimate the rate of return on capital as a function of certain predetermined variables, including tax variables. The second was to translate the regression coefficients of the tax variables into measures of the degree of shifting. In this connection, one must choose among various measures, all of which are logically valid but have different properties and may record different degrees of shifting for the same situation. This complicates matters, but must be made clear to avoid confusion.

Our study was launched in 1958–59 at the University of Michigan, resumed in 1960–61 at the Johns Hopkins University, and completed at Princeton and Wayne State University. It was made possible primarily by grants from the Merril Foundation for the Advancement of Financial Knowledge and from the National Science Foundation. Supplementary help was received also from the Ford Foundation Economic Research Programs of the University of Michigan and of the Johns Hopkins University, from the Brookings Institution, and from Wayne State University, especially its Computing and Data Processing Center, operating with the support of National Science Foundation grant number 19981. We express our thanks for this support and hope that the money was well invested.

Thanks are due also to Peter Briant, Ryuzo Sato, and Earl A. Spiller who participated in the project at earlier stages, and to many of our colleagues, especially Professors Carl Christ and Arthur Goldberger, who have contributed helpful suggestions.

Marian Krzyzaniak
Spring, 1963                               Richard A. Musgrave

# CONTENTS

# THE SHIFTING OF THE
# CORPORATION INCOME TAX

*An Empirical Study of its
Short-Run Effect upon the Rate of Return*

# CHAPTER 1

# INTRODUCTION

THE SHIFTING AND INCIDENCE of the corporation income tax have been theorized about at great length.[1] This discussion has been inconclusive, but a brief review of the main arguments will help in interpreting our empirical analysis.

To review the theoretical argument, we shall assume that the corporation tax is substituted for another tax of equal yield, thus permitting us to focus on differential incidence and to disregard the public-expenditure problem. Also, we shall assume that the tax substitution is in the context of a full-employment economy, thus permitting us to disregard effects on the level of employment, and to focus on the distribution, growth, and allocation aspects of the problem.

## Short-Run Adjustments

In the traditional approach, a distinction has been drawn between the short-run and the long-run effects of the tax. To avoid misunderstanding, it should be made clear just how these terms are to be used. Two sets of distinctions must be kept apart.

[1] The following items are but a sample of the long literature on this topic: F. Y. Edgeworth, *Papers Relating to Political Economy* (London: Macmillan & Co., Ltd., 1925), vol. II, p. 97; also see A. Cournot, *Researches into the Mathematical Principles of the Theory of Wealth*, ed. I. Fisher (New York: The Macmillan Co., 1938), p. 68 (first published 1838); Knut Wicksell, *Finanztheoretische Untersuchungen des Steuerwesen Schweden's* (Jena, Germany, 1896), pp. 11–20; Edwin R. Seligman, *Studies in Public Finance* (New York: The Macmillan Co., 1925), pp. 59–84; H. Dalton, *Principles of Public Finance* (9th ed.; London: Routledge & Kegan Paul, Ltd., 1936), pp. 81–85; Richard Goode, *Corporation Income Tax* (New York: John Wiley & Sons, 1951), pp. 47–54. Also see the Report of the Commission on National Debt and Taxation (Colwyn Report), (London: H. M. Stationery Office, 1927), Hansard 2700; D. H. Robertson, "The Colwyn Committee, the Income Tax and the Price Level," *Economic Journal*, vol. 37, no. 142, December, 1927, pp. 566–581, reprinted in R. A. Musgrave and Carl Shoup (eds.), *Readings in the Economics of Taxation*, American Economic Association (Homewood, Ill.: Irwin, 1958, pp. 297–311); W. H. Coates, "Incidence of the Income Tax," *Appendices to the Report of the Commission on National Debt and Taxation* (London: H. M. Stationery Office, 1927), pp. 65–113.

One distinction, theoretical in nature, is between effects which come about rapidly, and effects which are slow in working themselves out. The rapid type is referred to as "short-run" effects, and the period is set sufficiently short (one or two years) so as to exclude changes in capacity. The vehicle by which the "short-run" effects come about must thus be through changes in prices received or wages (or other cost payments) paid, with capacity constant. The slow type is referred to as "long-run" effects, and may come about only over a period sufficiently long to permit changes in capital stock, with corresponding adjustments in prices and costs.

Another distinction, observational in nature, is between results which show up if taxation effects are measured over a short period, as against results which show up only if a long period is examined. Long-run effects, as just defined, cannot show up in the first case; but short-run effects, as here defined, may prevail and be observed even if a longer period is examined. The "short-run" effect as here defined may thus have important consequences for the longer run; and if "long-run" effects are absent or unimportant, the "short-run" type of effects (which do not involve changes in capital stock) may indeed dominate even the observed long-run consequences of the tax.

Since the model here developed observes effects coming about within a year, and since fixed capital adjustments are hardly possible within that period, our results correspond to the theoretical concept of short-run effects.

Regarding the short-run effect, economists from Cournot on have argued that a profits tax will not affect optimum output under conditions of profit maximization, be it for monopoly or perfect competition. Consequently, prices and the gross (i.e., before tax) rate of return on capital must remain unchanged. This dictum was qualified later by recognition that taxable profits may contain variable cost elements, that changes in tax rates may act as a signal in oligopoly pricing, that the monopolist may use restraint in maximizing profits over the short run, aiming at a "fair" net (after tax) rate of return, that the profits tax may play a role in wage demands in collective bargaining, etc. All these elements may cause some degree of adjustment in prices or wages and may affect the gross rate of return. Short-run shifting may result from market imperfections, without contradiction with conventional price theory.

The businessman, however, has been skeptical regarding the entire approach of marginal cost pricing. His position has been that taxes are treated as a cost when determining prices, be it as part of a "full-cost-pricing" rule, by application of a conventional mark-up rate defined net of tax, or by pricing to meet a net of tax target rate of return. According to these formulae, a change in tax rate leads to an adjustment in price. The profits tax becomes a quasi sales tax. The fact that such a price policy is not consistent with the usual concepts of profit maximization does not disprove its existence. In all, it appears that the economist, speaking from his theoretical insight alone, cannot rule out the possibility of short-run shifting. Surprising or not, we shall find that our statistical results are compatible with the businessman's views.

## Long-Run Adjustments

While the traditional view holds that the short-run effect of the tax is to reduce profits and the rate of return, this reduction is then expected to depress capital formation in the long run. Thereby the burden may be spread from owners of capital to other groups. This raises two problems: First, there is the question whether and how the level of capital formation is reduced; and second, there is the question of how such reduction in the rate of capital formation as results will affect factor shares and the rate of return on capital.

Theoretical reasoning regarding the effects of a profits tax on the level of private capital formation is most difficult. It can be no more conclusive than is the underlying theory of investment behavior. Unfortunately, the state of this theory is quite unsatisfactory. Different hypotheses give different answers. If the investment function is taken to be of the accelerator type, then the tax effect can operate only through changing the level of total expenditures. In the full employment context investment can not be affected by the tax. If the investment function is of the propensity-to-invest type, taxation effects may operate via the resulting reduction in the internal supply of funds. These effects will be restrictive, but the resulting reduction in investment cannot exceed the tax yield. Using a profitability type of investment function, the tax effects may operate via effects on the rate of return. In this case, much depends on the nature of the tax, especially on the loss treatment, and it is by no means certain that investment will be curtailed.[2] However, if it is, the magnitude of the reduction in investment may exceed tax yield. Such effects as result are likely to require more than a year and may extend over several decades. Again, many outcomes are possible and the problem cannot be solved by theorizing alone.

Assume now that the tax does reduce the rate of capital formation. The resulting effects on factor incomes then depend on the form of the production

---

[2] See Evsey D. Domar and R. A. Musgrave, "Proportional Income Taxation and Risk Taking," *Quarterly Journal Of Economics*, vol. 58, May, 1944, pp. 387–422; and James E. Tobin, "Liquidity Preference as Behaviour Towards Risk," *Review of Economic Studies*, ser. 2, vol. 25, February, 1958, pp. 65–87.

function for a growing economy. If it is in the nature of a constant return to scale-type Cobb-Douglas function, factor shares will remain unchanged. At the same time, the rates of return to capital and labor will change, depending on the parameters of the system. Looked at in absolute terms, capital and wage incomes in future years will be below the level which would have been obtained under higher investment. What these results indicate with regard to "shifting" or "incidence" of the tax, depends on one's definition of these terms. For instance, if incidence is defined in terms of resulting changes in the *distribution* of income after tax, the tax may be said to stay put, since the profit share after tax has declined; but if incidence is defined in terms of changes in *absolute* income, labor bears part of the burden. The results become more complicated if we assume a non-Cobb-Douglas type of production function, in which case factor shares before tax may change as well.

*Complications*

The preceding discussion assumed that the corporation tax is a truly general tax on profits. This must now be corrected since (1) the tax applies in the corporate sector only, and (2) different treatment is given to earnings on equity and debt capital. Also, (3) there is the problem of separating tax effects from government expenditure effects.

1. Since the tax applies to the corporate sector only, it may induce a movement of capital from this sector to the unincorporated sector. Particular corporations may be disincorporated, or there may be a reallocation of capital toward industries which are characterized by unincorporated firms, i.e., capital may flow from manufacturing to real estate. The latter adjustment may be expected to occur over a longer period. As a result of such capital movement, the gross rate of return in the corporate sector may rise while that in the other sector falls.[3] In such a case, an isolated view of changes in

---

[3] This aspect is emphasized by Arnold C. Harberger in "The Incidence of the Corporation Tax," *The Journal of Political Economy*, vol. LXX, No. 3, June, 1962, pp. 215–40; and "The Corporation Income Tax: An Empirical Appraisal," in *Tax Revision Compendium*, vol. 1, Committee on Ways and Means, Nov. 16, 1959, pp. 231–51.

Without entering into an evaluation of Harberger's model, it may be useful at the outset to relate our analysis to his, even though this anticipates some of the later discussion:

1. Harberger's analysis is deductive, drawing conclusions regarding the consequence of the corporation tax from assumptions regarding market structure, production functions, etc. The analysis of this study takes an empirical approach, without a priori assumptions about market structure.

2. Harberger allows for a time sufficiently long for all necessary adjustments, including adjustments in capital (be it inter-industry movement or total), to occur. Our analysis attempts to measure the consequences of a tax rate change which come about within a

the gross rate of return in the corporate sector may suggest shifting. At the same time, there may have been no shifting in the more significant sense of passing the burden from the total (corporate plus unincorporated) capital share to the labor share or to the consumer. Even though capital flows readily in response to differential returns, the total capital supply may be inelastic, and changes in the total capital share which result from reallocation may be relatively minor. At the same time, by inducing capital movement to other industries, the tax may reduce the efficiency of resource allocation and give rise to an excess burden, such as is usually discussed in connection with partial excise taxes. Such a burden may result even though the total gross-profit share remains unchanged.

In appraising the importance of capital movement to the unincorporated sector, it should be noted that what matters is not the absolute level of corporation tax alone, but the difference between the total rates which the tax system as a whole imposes on the investor in the corporate and in the unincorporated sectors. This involves individual income tax rates, capital gains treatment, and other aspects of the tax system as well.

2. Since the tax permits deduction of interest on debt capital but does not allow deduction of imputed interest on equity capital, it may induce substitution of debt for equity finance. This may result in an increase in the gross rate of return on equity, so as to leave the net rate unchanged. At the same time, there may be no change in the gross rate of return on total capital, i.e., the

---

short period, i.e., a few years. Therefore, the effects of changes in capital stock in the corporate sector enter to a very limited degree only.

3. Harberger's assumptions of competitive market structure, and, if we read it correctly, even his interpretation of the monopoly case (in terms of mark-up rather than factors such as restrained monopoly or oligopoly pricing) are hard to reconcile with our statistical results, or vice versa. If there is a quick and persistent recoupment of the tax prior to capital adjustments, the need for reduction of capital in the corporate sector and for equalization with other sectors (which is the essence of Harberger's analysis) is diminished.

4. An excess burden problem, though in somewhat different form, may arise whether price changes through the Harberger mechanism or through revision of administered prices, as implied by our results.

5. Harberger de-emphasizes the possibility that total capital formation is depressed by the fall in the net rate of return (all sectors) which results in his system. But suppose such a result would follow. Then the implications for total capital formation and growth differ greatly, depending on whether an observed price rise in the corporate sector reflects (a) the rate of return being restored by "administered" price and/or wage changes, in which case the net rate of returns is not reduced to begin with and no adverse effects on capital formation result; or (b) the net rate of return being equalized with the non-corporate sector through inter-sector capital flows, in which case total capital formation is retarded. This point seems to be missed in a recent statement by the Committee for Economic Development. See *Reducing Tax Rates for Production and Economic Growth*, Committee for Economic Development, Dec., 1962, p. 22.

ratio of profits plus debt. As far as effects on the distribution of total income between capital and wage income are concerned, there has been no shifting. At the same time the position of investors in equity will have suffered relative to that of investors in debt. The net rate of return per unit of risk taking enjoyed by equity holders will decline relative to that enjoyed by bond holders;[4] and the ratio of profits after tax to interest payments will fall. Moreover, a further type of excess burden may arise.

The importance of these complications in the concrete setting of the U.S. corporation tax depends on how readily the unincorporated form of enterprise may be substituted for the corporate form, how readily capital may move to the unincorporated sector, and how readily debt finance may be substituted for equity finance. It may well be that these choices are determined largely by non-tax factors,[5] so that these two types of structural adjustments are relatively unimportant. Nevertheless, they must be kept in mind, especially when interpreting the behavior of various indicators of shifting.

3. In analyzing various taxation effects—be it the broader problem of incidence or the narrower issue of resulting changes in the rate of return— the question always remains how such effects can be separated from the effects of other elements of budget policy.[6] In theoretical reasoning, one may consider the results of changing a particular tax rate while holding public expenditures and other taxes constant. This concept of "absolute" effect serves the purpose of focusing on the specific tax change. But placed in a general equilibrium context, it is awkward because it implies aggregate-demand effects and resulting changes in price level or employment. This difficulty may be avoided by considering simultaneous changes in the tax rate and in public expenditures. This concept of "budget" effect in turn has the disadvantage of mixing tax and expenditure effects, which is not the most interesting problem. A final possibility is to hold expenditures constant and to examine the effects of tax substitution. This approach of "differential" effect may be the most satisfactory formulation of the problem, from a theoretical point of view.

The empirical results of our theoretical model do not fall neatly into any of these concepts. To begin with, it would be hardly possible to construct a

---

[4] See Franco Modigliani and M. H. Miller, "The Cost of Capital, Corporation Finance and the Theory of Investment," *The American Economic Review*, vol. XLVIII, June, 1958, pp. 261–97.

[5] With regard to choice of financing instruments, this view is arrived at by M. H. Miller, "The Corporation Income Tax and Corporate Financial Policies," *Research Paper*, prepared for Commission on Money and Credit.

[6] See R. A. Musgrave, *The Theory of Public Finance* (New York: McGraw-Hill, 1959), Chap. 10.

model measuring "differential" effects. The best we can do is to aim at "absolute" effects, but even this proves difficult. It happens that changes in the corporate tax rate were highly correlated with public expenditure changes, making it difficult to isolate the two effects, and leaving us with a result which may come closer to that of budget effects than that of absolute corporation tax effects. To a lesser degree, this problem arises also with regard to changes in other taxes.

# CHAPTER 2

# A PRELIMINARY VIEW

THERE HAVE BEEN a number of attempts in recent years to draw empirical conclusions on incidence, based on the observation of various time series. pertaining to profits, rates of return, and shares in national income.[1] These changes are then imputed to tax effects and taken as an indication of shifting. In interpreting the observed changes in these indicators, it must be kept in mind that there are many influences at work other than the tax factor, and that without isolating the latter, only a crude impression can be gained. The purpose of this study is precisely to undertake an attempt at such isolation, but by way of introduction, a brief look at the general picture will be useful. Even here, it is important to define how shifting is to be measured.

The concepts of "shifting" and "incidence" are not easily defined and mean different things to different people. For the immediate purposes of this chapter, we need only to say that "shifting" of the corporation tax relates to the recovery of the burden which the tax imposes on the taxpayer, the "burden"

---

[1] For a discussion of recent work along these lines see B. U. Ratchford and P. B. Han, "The Burden of the Corporate Income Tax," *National Tax Journal*, Vol. X, No. 4, December, 1957, pp. 310–24.

Also, see M. A. Adelman, "The Corporate Income Tax in the Long Run," *Journal of Political Economy*, LXV, April, 1957, p. 152; Morris Beck, "Ability to Shift the Corporate Income Tax: Seven Industrial Groups," *National Tax Journal*, III, September, 1950, pp. 248, 253–56; E. Cary Brown, "The Corporate Income Tax in the Short Run," *National Tax Journal*, VII, September, 1954, pp. 240–41; John C. Clendenin, "Effect of Corporate Income Taxes on Corporate Earnings," *Taxes*, XXXIV, June, 1956, p. 396; Richard Goode, "Some Consideration on the Incidence of the Corporation Income Tax," *Journal of Finance*, VI, June, 1951, p. 197; Eugene M. Lerner, and Eldon S. Hendriksen, "Federal Taxes on Corporate Income and the Rate of Return on Investment in Manufacturing, 1927 to 1952," *National Tax Journal*, VIII, September, 1956, pp. 199, 202; John Lintner, "Effects of a Shifted Corporate Income Tax on Real Investment," *National Tax Journal*, VIII, September, 1955, p. 235; Merton H. Miller, and John P. Shelton, "Effects of a Shifted Corporate Income Tax on Capital Structure," *National Tax Journal*, VIII, September, 1955, p. 256; Richard A. Musgrave, J. J. Carrol, L. D. Cook, and L. Frane, "Distribution of Tax Payments by Income Groups: A Case Study for 1948," *National Tax Journal*, IV, March, 1951, p. 14–16; Carl S. Shoup, "Some Considerations of the Incidence of the Corporation Income Tax," *Journal of Finance*, VI, June, 1951, p. 187; J. Fred Weston, "Incidence and Effects of the Corporate Income Tax," *National Tax Journal*, II, December, 1949, pp. 307, 309, 312, 315.

being the difference in his position as it is with the tax and as it would have been without the tax. The difference may be measured in terms of various "indicators," such as absolute profits, rates of return, or share in national income. The degree to which the potential burden (i.e., the burden which would result in the absence of any adjustment on the taxpayer's part) is avoided or recovered, indicates the "degree of shifting."[2]

## A. INDICATORS OF SHIFTING

We assume for the time being that the effect of the tax factor on the various "indicators" has been isolated and consider what their movement tells us about shifting.

### *Types of Indicators*

Various possible indicators, most of which have been used in recent discussions, may be arranged as follows:

Table 2–1. Indicators of Shifting

| Sector | Tax-induced change in | Absolute amounts | Rates of return on capital of | | Shares in value added of | |
|---|---|---|---|---|---|---|
| | | | Corporations | All business | Corporations | All business |
| Corporations only | Profits only | 1 | 5 | – | 9 | 11 |
| | All capital earnings | 2 | 6 | – | 10 | 12 |
| All business | Profits only | 3 | – | 7 | – | 13 |
| | All capital earnings | 4 | – | 8 | – | 14 |

A first way of looking at the problem is in terms of absolute profits according to indicators 1–4. For obvious reasons this is less instructive than observation of changes in rates of return or factor shares. The insight to be gained with regard to shifting from the historical pattern of financial data, such as given in this chapter, altogether depends on the validity of assuming that non-tax influences were absent on balance. This assumption is clearly absurd in the case of absolute profits, if only for the reason that the capital stock grows

---

[2] For further conceptual discussion, see Chap. 5 and Appendix C.

over time. It is less so regarding ratios such as rate of return or factor share which are at least partially self-correcting.

The rate of return indicator is of major interest because it may be presumed that investment activity depends on the rate of return, with its consequences for the level of capital formation, capital allocation, and growth.[3] This is formulated most broadly in indicator 8 by relating all capital earnings (profits plus interest paid) to all capital. If the tax effect is to reduce the net rate of return, then investment as a whole has become less profitable. A quite narrow view of this relationship is given in indicator 5 by relating corporate profits to corporate equity. The effect of the tax on this rate of return clearly does not tell the whole story. By inducing debt finance or capital flow into unincorporated business, the profitability of investment may be restricted somewhere else. These effects are partially accounted for by indicators 6 or 7.

The share indicator is of interest primarily because it relates to the distributional effects of the tax.[4] The most comprehensive picture is given by indicator 14, which relates total capital earnings to total value added by business. If the tax reduces the share of capital, and if the capital share is distributed less equally by size groups than the labor share, then the tax tends to reduce income inequality. No such definite conclusion can be drawn if a narrower view of the share is taken, as in indicator 9. Indicators 10 to 13 again allow for varying degrees of comprehensiveness of the picture.

If one considers a period so short that capital is held constant, the absolute profit and rate of return indicators are in full agreement. If there are no non-tax factors affecting value added, there will also be a general agreement with the movement of share indicators. In the longer run, the absolute profit indicators are useless, while rate of return and share indicators may differ widely. Moreover, quite different time periods may be involved in the working out of effects on total capital formation, value added, intersector movements, and changes in type of finance.

It should be noted that these indicators do not tell us by what *mechanism* the shifting process comes about. To study the mechanism of shifting in the short run, changes in prices ("forward" shifting), in wages ("backward" shifting), and perhaps in profit margins are relevant, as well as inter-sector movements of capital and changes in financial structure. To examine the process of shifting in the long run, changes in investment and effects on productivity are relevant. In interpreting our approach to the problem, these

---

[3] Those who hold that investment depends on internal funds may prefer to examine effects on the ratio of profits plus depreciation to capital.

[4] The definition of distributional consequences in terms of changes in factor shares deals with changes from the earnings side of relative income positions only. To gain a complete picture, tax effects on relative prices and resulting changes from the income uses side would have to be considered as well. See Musgrave, *The Theory of Public Finance*, Chap. 10.

factors underlying the mechanism of shifting had to be kept in mind; but for the time being, our concern is merely with the indicators as end results.

## Zero and 100 Per Cent Shifting

We now define what constitutes zero and 100 per cent shifting under the various indicators,

Table 2–2. Conditions of Zero and 100 Per Cent Shifting

| Indicator | Zero shifting | 100% shifting |
|---|---|---|
| Absolute profit (gross terms) | $\pi_g = \pi'$ | $\pi_n = (1 - Z)\pi_g = \pi'$ |
| Rate of return (gross terms) | $Y_g = Y'$ | $Y_n = (1 - Z)Y_g = Y'$ |
| Net share | $F_n = (1 - Z)F'$ | $F_n = F'$ |
| Gross share | $F_g = F'$ | $(1 - Z)F_g = F'$ |

where $\pi$ is profits, $Y$ is the rate of return, $F$ is the profit share, and $Z$ is the tax rate. Throughout this study, the term "*gross* return" will be used to indicate return before deducting tax, and "*net* return" will be used to indicate return after deducting tax. Subscript $g$ indicates gross and subscript $n$ indicates net such that $\pi_n = (1 - Z)\pi_g$ by definition. Priming means value in absence of tax. The problem of how to define the degrees of shifting other than 0 to 100 per cent is more complicated and will be considered later.[5]

The definitions for the absolute profit and rate-of-return indicators are self explanatory. They are here stated in gross terms, but may be translated without change in meaning into net terms.[6]

The case of the share indicator is more difficult. An easy solution to the problem would be to take the absolute profit or rate-of-return definitions and translate them into share terms.[7] This, however, would be of no value because

[5] See Chap. 5 and Appendix C.

[6] We then have

| Indicator | Zero Shifting | 100% Shifting |
|---|---|---|
| Absolute profit (net terms) | $\pi_n = (1 - Z)\pi'$ | $\pi_n = \pi'$ |
| Rate of return (net terms) | $Y_n = (1 - Z)Y'$ | $Y_n = Y'$ |

[7] Using the absolute profit indicator and assuming a system where profits $(\pi)$ and wages $(W)$ are the only two shares, we have

| Indicator | Zero Shifting | 100% Shifting Forward | Backward |
|---|---|---|---|
| Net share | $F_n = \dfrac{\pi' - T}{\pi' - T + W'}$ | $F_n = F'$ | $F_n = \dfrac{\pi'}{\pi' + W' - T}$ |
| Gross share | $F_g = F'$ | $F_g = \dfrac{\pi' + T}{\pi' + T + W'}$ | $F_g = F' + \dfrac{T}{\pi' + W'}$ |

where the net profit share is $F_n = \dfrac{\pi_n}{\pi_n + W}$ and the gross profit share $F_g = \dfrac{\pi_g}{\pi_g + W}$. It will be noted that this formulation gives different gross measures for 100 per cent shifting, depending on the direction of shifting. This direction must be known, therefore, to interpret the observed change in shares.

it would merely be a reformulation of the earlier concepts. The problem is to find definitions for the share indicator which are meaningful in terms of share analysis. Looking at the matter in this way, it appears that for the share case there is a substantive difference between the net and gross formulation.

One purpose of the share approach to shifting is to examine distributional implications. The relevant issue here seems to be the change in the distribution of income after tax or the change in the net profit share $F_n$. Assuming an economy with two factor shares, profits $\pi$ and wages $W$, and a profits tax only, we have $F_n = \dfrac{\pi_n}{\pi_n + W}$. This readily suggests that 100 per cent shifting be defined as a situation where $F_n = F'$. In other words, the share of profits in value added available for private use remains unchanged. Similarly one may define zero shifting as a situation where the share of profits in value added available for private use is reduced by the rate of tax, this is to say $F_n = (1 - Z)F'$.

Another purpose of the share approach is to consider what has happened to factor shares in the context of national income and factor-price analysis. What is relevant here is the change in the gross share $F_g$, where $F_g = \dfrac{\pi_g}{\pi_g + W}$. Now we have a ready definition of zero shifting as $F_g = F'$, a situation where the profit share (including tax) in total value added remains constant. Correspondingly, we define 100 per cent shifting as $(1 - Z)F_g = F'$, a situation where the share of profits (including tax) in total value added rises by the tax share in total value added.

While both these share indicators are independent of the "direction" of shifting, the movement of profits and of the rate of return for any given degree of shifting depend on its direction. Such is the case because a given behavior of the profit share may be the net result of many different pairs of wage and profit changes.[8]

---

[8] This is shown in the following table which gives the required value of $\pi_n$, net profit after tax, for the various indicators. $T$ is the tax liability equal to $Z\pi_g$.

In reading Table 2–3, note that zero shifting in the share sense does not exclude wage or price adjustments leading to changes in absolute profits and to shifting in terms of the absolute profit indicator. Indeed, we find that net profits must decline if there is to be zero shifting in the share sense. The extent of the required decline depends on the direction of the shifting. For all but one case (zero shifting according to the gross-share indicator, with forward adjustment), the required decline in net profits exceeds that for zero shifting under the absolute profit indicator. Also it may be noted that the required $\pi_n$ is larger

## B. THE EVIDENCE

We now turn to the historical evidence provided by the various indicators. Over the last decades, tax rates have risen sharply, and it is interesting to consider what have been concurrent changes in factor shares and rates of return on capital. These changes, as noted before, are the result of many forces, including (but by no means only) tax influences. Since the latter are not isolated, only crude conclusions on tax influences can be drawn. This gives additional reason to prefer the general indicators, especially indicators 8 and 14 of Table 2–1, where non-tax influences on inter-sectional and inter-financial movements will not distort the picture.

### *Absolute Level of Profits*

Simple observation of the absolute level of corporation gross profits, corresponding to indicator 1 of Table 2–1, is altogether misleading. The *caeteris paribus* assumption in this case is entirely untenable, the absolute level of profits having been affected by powerful non-tax factors, such as the increase in capital stock due to growth.

Nevertheless, the absolute profit picture may be considered briefly. Gross profits rose from $10 billion in the late twenties to over $40 billion in the fifties. Corporation tax rates rose from 10 to 52 per cent, liabilities rose from over $1 billion to over $20 billion, and profits after tax rose from $8 billion to $25 billion. For 100 per cent shifting, and given the *caeteris paribus* assump-

---

with forward than with backward adjustment, and that given the direction of adjustment, the required $\pi_n$ for the gross-share measure is larger than for the net-share measure.

Table 2–3. Conditions of Zero and 100 Per Cent Shifting Under Share Indicators Stated in Terms of Net Profits

| Indicator | Required value of net profits $\pi_n$ for | |
|---|---|---|
| | Zero per cent shifting | 100 per cent shifting |
| 1. Net share | | |
|   a) adjustment backward $(W = W' - T)$ | $\left(1 - \dfrac{2T}{W'}\right)\pi' - T$ | $\left(1 - \dfrac{T}{W'}\right)\pi'$ |
|   b) adjustment forward $(W = W')$ | $\left(1 - \dfrac{T}{W'}\right)\pi' - T$ | $\pi'$ |
| 2. Gross share | | |
|   a) adjustment backward $(W = W' - T)$ | $\left(1 - \dfrac{T}{W'}\right)\pi' - T$ | $\pi'$ |
|   b) adjustment forward $(W = W')$ | $\pi' - T$ | $\left(1 + \dfrac{T}{W'}\right)\pi'$ |

tion, gross profits should have increased from $10 billion to $29 billion.[9] The observed increase having been to $40 billion, shifting would have been much above 100 per cent. Defining the degree of shifting as the ratio of actual increase in gross profits (corrected for initial tax rate) to the increase needed for full recovery of the additional burden due to the rise in tax rate, one would arrive at shifting of 157 per cent.[10] All this has no meaning, however, since other influences were clearly present.

### Profit Share

Changes in gross shares are shown in Table 2–4, corresponding to indicators 9 to 14 of Table 2–1. While the more general indicators 11–14 would again be preferable on conceptual grounds, the data for the non-incorporated sector are much less reliable than those for the incorporated sector. On these grounds, indicators 9 and 10 are to be preferred. Indicator 10 includes interest income on debt capital, measured here as interest paid by the corporate sector to the outside. It thus has the advantage that tax effects on the financial structure are neutralized; but it has the disadvantage that non-tax effects on interest income from debt capital are included.

We begin with indicator 9. The most meaningful comparison, perhaps, is that between 1922–29 and 1948–57, as both represent periods of high employment. Over this period the corporation tax rate rose from about 10 to 52 per cent. The gross share or corporation profits as a per cent of corporate value added rose from 19.2 to 22.6 per cent. Full shifting would have required an increase to 27 per cent. The data needed for estimating the implicit degree

---

[9] The condition for 100 per cent shifting was defined previously (Table 2–2) as $\pi_g - \pi' = Z\pi_g$. Since we are now dealing with an increase in tax rates, we must compare the equilibrium with 100 per cent shifting at the new tax rate $Z_1$ with that at the old tax rate $Z_0$.

Thus $$\pi_{g,1} - \pi' = Z_1\pi_{g,1}$$
and $$\pi_{g,0} - \pi' = Z_0\pi_{g,0}$$

Deducting the second from the first equation, we obtain

$$\pi_{g,1} - \pi_{g,0} = \pi_{g,1}Z_1 - \pi_{g,0}Z_0$$

as the condition for 100 per cent shifting of the incremental tax rate.

[10] The formula for 100 per cent shifting in the preceding note suggest that the degree of shifting $S$ be defined as

$$S = \frac{\pi_{g,1} - \pi_{g,0}}{\pi_{g,1}Z_1 - \pi_{g,0}Z_0} = \frac{\pi_{g,1} - \pi_{g,0}}{T_1 - T_0} \qquad \text{if } T = Z\pi_g$$

See p. 37, where this formula is used for $Z_0 = 0$.

Table 2–4.  Factor Shares (Gross) in Income Originating in Corporate and Total Business Sections

| No. | Indicator | 1922–29[b] | 1929[c] | 1930–39[c] | 1936–39[c] | 1940–49[c] | 1948–57[c] |
|-----|-----------|-----------|--------|-----------|-----------|-----------|-----------|
| | As percent of corporate value added: | | | | | | |
| 9 | Corporate profits before tax | 19.2 | 21.8 | 9.8 | 14.8 | 23.8 | 22.6 |
| 10 | Corporate profits before tax plus interest paid by corporations to non-corporate sector | 23.0 | 25.4 | 15.4 | 19.2 | 24.7 | 22.8 |
| | As percent of total value added by business:[a] | | | | | | |
| 11 | Corporate profits before tax | – | 14.3 | 6.3 | 9.6 | 15.5 | 15.7 |
| 12 | Corporate profits before tax plus interest | – | 16.6 | 9.9 | 12.4 | 16.1 | 15.8 |
| 13 | Corporate profits before tax and income of unincorporated business | – | 35.5 | 27.0 | 31.1 | 37.3 | 33.2 |
| 14 | Corporate profits before tax, income of unincorporated business and total interest paid | – | 38.8 | 32.0 | 34.7 | 38.2 | 33.6 |

ᵃ Unincorporated business does not include operations of mutuals, co-operatives, trade associations, and non-profit organizations.
  ᵇ Source: H. D. Osborne and J. B. Epstein, Corporate Profits Since World War I, *Survey of Current Business*, U.S. Department of Commerce, Jan. 1956, pp. 8–20.
  ᶜ Source: *U.S. Income and Output, A Supplement to the Survey of Current Business.* U.S. Department of Commerce, 1958, Table 1–12, pp. 134–35, National Income and Gross National Product by legal form of organization, 1929–57.

of shifting are hardly available, but a rough calculation suggests 44 per cent.[11] Indicator 10, which includes interest income, shows approximately zero shifting for the period. This is the particular result which is featured in Adelman's study.[12] The result of lower shifting with inclusion of interest income is in line with the hypothesis that the increase in tax has induced substitution of debt for equity finance. But again, the *caeteris paribus* assumption does not hold. The interest share in fact declined rather than rose, due largely to a decline in interest rates. There was only a minor substitution of

---

[11] In line with the gross share definition in Table 2–2 the formula for the degree of shifting (gross share) is

$$S_g = \frac{F_{g,1} - F_{g,0}}{\dfrac{T_1}{\pi_{g,1} + W_1} - \dfrac{T_0}{\pi_{g,0} + W_0}}$$

For full shifting $S_g = 1$.
  In arriving at the ratios of 27 and 44 per cent, we estimated first the ratio of tax to corporate value added for 1922–29. The values for $\pi_g$ and $T$ are obtained from *Statistics of Income* for the years 1922–29. They are then scaled from 1929 back so as to agree in 1929 with figures from *U.S. Income and Output, op. cit.* See also p. 65 for a further estimate of share shifting. Using the gross shares as given by Osborne and Epstein, *op. cit.* we arrive at the non-profit income. The data for 1948–57 are given in *U.S. Income and Output, op. cit.*
  [12] See Adelman, *op. cit.*

debt for equity finance; and such substitution as occurred appears to have been due to non-tax factors.[13] Though indicator 10 may be conceptually better, the evidence of indicator 9 seems preferable because we know that certain additional *caeteris paribus* assumptions implicit in indicator 10 do not hold.

The share picture, pertaining to indicators 11–14 does not permit comparison with the twenties and, as noted before, the data for the unincorporated sector are less satisfactory. However, the general picture seems to be fairly similar to that for the corporate sector, thus not supporting the hypothesis of a strong tax-induced shift between sectors.[14]

So far, reference has been to gross shares only. The net picture, though more interesting, is more difficult to come by. Corporate profits after tax as a per cent of corporate value added net of tax are estimated at 16.0 per cent for 1922–29 and at 12.7 per cent for 1948–57.[15] A heroic estimate suggests that this implies shifting of 42 per cent,[16] which is only slightly below that for the gross share picture.

### Rates of Return

Changes in the rate of return are shown in Table 2–5. These correspond to indicators 5 and 6 of Table 2–1.

The table is given in terms of net rates of return, because (given the *caeteris paribus* assumption) *any* increase in the net rate suggests shifting in excess of 100 per cent, a result which holds for most cases. The results are shown for a "total capital base" (ratio of profits plus interest paid to equity plus interest bearing debt) and for an "equity base" (ratio of profits to net worth).

The case of all manufacturing corporations, total capital base, is shown in line 2 of Table 2–5. The increase in the net rate or return was 11 per cent when comparing the late twenties with the mid-fifties, and 36 per cent when the base is the late thirties. In both cases shifting exceeded 100 per cent. This is in line with the results obtained by Lerner and Hendriksen.[17] In order

---

[13] See Merton Miller, "The Corporation Income Tax and Corporate Financial Policies," *op. cit.*

[14] This is in line with our conclusions for the differential-rate approach. See p. 57.

[15] The additional information needed is net-profits, which for the 1922–29 period were obtained by deducting adjusted tax liability from adjusted gross profits as derived in note 11, p. 15 for gross shares.

[16] In line with the net-share of definition of Table 2–2, the formula for the degree of shifting (see p. 11) is now

$$S_n = 1 + \frac{F_{n,1} - F_{n,0}}{Z_1 F_{n,0} - Z_0 F_{n,1}}$$

[17] See Lerner and Hendriksen, *op. cit.*

Table 2–5. Net Rates of Return after Tax[a]
All Corporations and All Manufacturing

| No. | Description | Average (Percent) | | | Percentage Change From | |
|---|---|---|---|---|---|---|
| | | 1927–29 | 1936–39 | 1955–57 | 1927–29 to 1955–57 | 1936–39 to 1955–57 |
| 1. | Statutory tax rate | 11 to 13.5 | 15 to 19 | 52.0 | 40.0 | 35.0 |
| 2. | All manufacturing, total capital base | | | | | |
| | Rate of return after tax | 7.6 | 6.3 | 8.5 | 11.2 | 35.6 |
| | Turnover | 109.0 | 118.5 | 195.0 | 78.8 | 64.5 |
| | Margin | 6.9 | 5.2 | 4.3 | −37.8 | −16.3 |
| 3. | All manufacturing, equity base | | | | | |
| | Rate of return after tax | 8.0 | 6.3 | 9.4 | 18.2 | 50.6 |
| | Turnover | 134.7 | 113.0 | 240.8 | 78.8 | 113.2 |
| | Margin | 5.9 | 4.6 | 3.9 | −33.8 | −14.7 |
| 4. | All manufacturing, equity base Adjusted for price change (inventory valuation profits excluded) | | | | | |
| | Rate of return after tax | n.c.[b] | 6.5 | 6.3 | n.c.[b] | −2.1 |
| | Turnover | n.c.[b] | 141.4 | 225.1 | n.c.[b] | 59.1 |
| | Margin | n.c.[b] | 4.7 | 2.8 | n.c.[b] | −40.2 |
| 5. | All manufacturing, equity base Adjusted for price change (inventory valuation profits included) | | | | | |
| | Rate of return after tax | 7.8 | 6.7 | 7.3 | −6.5 | 9.0 |
| | Turnover | 135.4 | 141.4 | 225.1 | 66.3 | 59.1 |
| | Margin | 5.8 | 4.6 | 3.2 | −43.9 | −30.1 |
| 6. | All corporations, equity base | | | | | |
| | Rate of return after tax | 7.0 | 4.0 | 7.5 | 20.5 | 87.5 |
| | Turnover | 85.7 | 69.8 | 176.6 | 106.0 | 152.8 |
| | Margin | 8.2 | 5.6 | 4.8 | −41.8 | −15.2 |

[a] For sources see Chapter 3, Section B
[b] Inventory valuation adjustment series not available

to determine degrees of shifting, it is more convenient to proceed from changes in the gross rates of return,[18] shown for certain key cases in Table 2–6. The degrees of shifting on the total capital base are 107 and 134 per cent for the two periods respectively.

As before, the results cannot be taken at face value because non-tax factors did not remain constant. However, it is of interest to see how the change in the rate of return was reflected in changes in margins and in the rate of turnover. The net rate of return is the product of net margin and turnover, so that

$$Y_n = \frac{S}{K} \frac{\pi_n}{S}$$

where $Y_n$ is net rate of return, $\pi_n$ is net profit, $S$ is sales, and $K$ is capital.

[18] Unlike for the share indicator, the gross or net approach now gives the same degree of shifting, but computation is simpler in gross terms. See p. 83.

$S/K$ is turnover and the ratio $\frac{\pi_n}{S}$ is net margin. Comparing 1927–29 with 1955–57, we find that the 11 per cent rise in $Y_n$ was accompanied by a 79 per cent rise in turnover and a decline in net margins by 38 per cent. Suppose now that the *caeteris paribus* assumption holds. What does the rise in turnover and drop in net margin tell us about the process of shifting? If, on the one hand, the shifting had been accomplished through price rise, given inelastic private demand for the total corporate product and increased government outlays, it would have increased sales, thus raising turnover. Since $Y_n$ did not rise appreciably, this would have lowered margins. Thus, the observed rise in turnover and decline in margins are compatible. If, on the other hand, the tax was not recouped by price rise, the decline in the margin could have been balanced by an increase in turnover due to retardation in capital formation. Thus, the evidence is compatible with various types of adjustments. Moreover, the picture is far from conclusive, since many other factors operating on margins and turnover did not remain constant.

The general picture does not change greatly if we consider equity finance only. As shown in line 3 of Table 2–5, the increase in the rate of return is greater, as is the degree of shifting shown in Table 2–6. The degrees of shifting

Table 2–6. Degrees of Shifting, All Manufacturing[a]

| No. | Description | Average gross rate of return as percentage | | | Shifting[b] | |
|---|---|---|---|---|---|---|
| | | 1927–29 | 1936–39 | 1955–57 | 1955–57 to 1927–29 | 1955–57 to 1936–39 |
| 1. | Equity base | 8.7 | 7.9 | 18.9 | 1.239 | 1.362 |
| 2. | Total capital base | 8.1 | 7.5 | 16.1 | 1.070 | 1.344 |
| 3. | Equity base, adjusted for price change (inventory valuation profits excluded) | – | 7.9 | 15.2 | – | .985 |
| 4. | Equity base, adjusted for price change (inventory valuation profits included) | 8.6 | 8.2 | 16.2 | .999 | 1.138 |
| 5. | Equity base, companies with assets under 50 M | – | 7.8 | 16.9 | – | 1.243 |
| 6. | Equity base, companies with assets over 50 M | – | 8.1 | 20.2 | – | 1.406 |
| 7. | 15 largest manufacturing companies (price leaders) | – | 10.9 | 27.5 | – | 1.468 |
| 8. | 15 largest manufacturing companies (price followers) | – | 11.5 | 25.5 | – | 1.402 |
| 9. | 26 steel companies | – | 9.0 | 26.9 | – | 1.568 |
| 10. | 12 textile companies | – | 9.6 | 10.3 | – | .2136 |
| 11. | Average rate of statutory tax | 10.0 | 17.0 | 52.0 | – | – |

[a] The formula is: $S_{01} = \dfrac{Y_{g,1} - Y_{g,0}}{Y_{g,1}Z_1 - Y_{g,0}Z_0} = \dfrac{Y_{g,1} - Y_{g,0}}{L_1 - L_0}$ where $L$ is tax liability divided by capital.

[b] Effective rates used to estimate shifting.

for the two periods are now 124 and 136 per cent respectively. The difference in the behavior of the rate of return on equity and total capital reflects a slight rise in the debt to equity ratio (with debt yield being lower than equity yield), as well as a rise in equity yield relative to debt yield.

The reader may wonder whether the "true" rise in the rate of return is not overstated by failure to allow for inflation and by inclusion of inventory valuation profits, thereby giving a misleading impression of high shifting. To test this hypothesis, the data were adjusted to correct for inflation,[19] as shown in lines 4 and 5 of Table 2–5. The increase in the net rates of return is dampened, with shifting falling slightly short of 100 per cent for the period 1927–29 to 1955–57 and slightly exceeding 100 per cent for the period 1936–39 to 1955–57. The corresponding degrees of shifting as shown in Table 2–6 are 98 and 114 per cent. While allowance for inflation dampened the results somewhat, it does not change the picture of heavy shifting.[20]

Turning now from manufacturing to all corporations (equity base), we find (line 6 of Table 2–5) that the rise in the rate of return from the twenties to the fifties was similar to that for manufacturing only. However, for the later period the increase for all corporations was much greater, suggesting shifting (given the *caeteris paribus* assumption) of nearly 200 per cent.

Changes in the rate of return for various subgroups (chosen to permit comparison with our later analysis) are shown in Table 2–7. The comparison

Table 2–7. Net Rates of Return after Tax[a]
Subgroups of All Manufacturing

| No. | Description | Average | | Percentage change from |
|---|---|---|---|---|
| | | 1936–39 | 1955–57 | 1936–39 to 1955–57 |
| | All manufacturing, equity base | | | |
| 1. | Companies with assets up to $50 M | 6.3 | 8.1 | +28.1 |
| 2. | Companies with assets over $50 M | 6.8 | 10.3 | +51.6 |
| | Industry groups, total capital base | | | |
| 3. | Pulp and paper | 5.0 | 9.1 | +82.2 |
| 4. | Rubber and products | 5.6 | 9.2 | +64.0 |
| 5. | Leather, hide, and products | 3.7 | 6.5 | +77.5 |
| 6. | Food and kindred products | 5.9 | 7.2 | +23.1 |
| 7. | Stone, clay, and glass | 6.6 | 10.8 | +64.3 |
| | Industry samples, equity base | | | |
| 8. | 26 steel companies | 7.1 | 13.6 | +90.8 |
| 9. | 12 textile companies | 7.6 | 5.1 | −33.1 |
| 10. | 15 largest manufacturing companies (price leaders) | 9.1 | 14.4 | +58.4 |
| 11. | 15 largest manufacturing companies (price followers) | 9.4 | 13.4 | +42.9 |

[a] For sources, see Chapter 3, Section B

[19] For methods of adjustment, see p. 76.

[20] For a discussion of the significance of the inflation adjustment for shifting see p. 56.

by asset-size groups indicates shifting in excess of 100 per cent for both groups, but a somewhat higher degree of shifting for the larger group. As shown in Table 2–6, the degrees of shifting are 124 per cent for the smaller and 141 per cent for the larger group. This would seem to be in line with the hypothesis that shifting is facilitated by strength of market position. Individual industry groups on the total capital base all show shifting in excess of 100 per cent, but with wide variation. The samples of individual firms in the steel industry, computed on the equity base, show shifting well in excess of 100 per cent, while those in textiles fall far short of full shifting. Our sample for the 15 largest companies tending to be price leaders show high shifting, in line with the picture for all companies with assets over $50 million. Again these results cannot be taken at face value, as they are altogether subject to the assumption that non-tax influences were absent.

### Conclusion

If the various indicators are interpreted on the extreme assumption that non-tax influences were totally absent, we find shifting under the profit and rate-of-return approaches to be 100 per cent for all-manufacturing and most of its subgroups. At the same time, shifting in all-manufacturing under the share approach is below 50 per cent. Discarding the absolute profits indicator as meaningless, how could one reconcile the results (in the context of the *caeteris paribus* assumption) for the rate of return and the share approaches?

Since the comparisons cover a span from 20 to 30 years, both "short" (quick) and "long-run" (slow) types of adjustments may have occurred. For instance, the tax might have reduced the net rate of return in the short run, shifting being initially less than 100 per cent. This retarded capital formation, thereby holding down the profit share but allowing the rate of return to rise. This interpretation is more or less in line (not entirely, since the gross capital share rose somewhat) with a Cobb-Douglas type of production function with perfectly competitive markets and an elastic capital supply. As will be seen later, this explanation is not supported by our short-run analysis. An alternative interpretation, supported by this analysis, is that the rate of return was pushed up in response to the tax by short-run types of adjustments, thus involving short-run shifting, and that this had no effect on factor inputs, but that the nature of the production function was such that the gross capital share would have declined in absence of tax. Other explanations involving changes in various factor inputs may also apply.

Altogether different explanations may be developed if the *caeteris paribus* assumption is dropped. Non-tax factors such as changes in market structure might have occurred. If we add the hypothesis that rising union strength tended to depress the gross rate of return, reconciliation of the results becomes even harder and strengthens the presumption that substantial shifting of the short-run type occurred. The alternative hypothesis of structural changes favoring capital helps the explanation and reduces the need for postulating high short-run shifting. But these other changes would have had to be very large to sustain the assumption of zero short-run shifting.

It appears that there are many ways of interpreting the results for the particular indicators, and of reconciling them with each other. General observation of the data leaves the impression that there probably has been substantial shifting, even in the short run, but no definite conclusion is possible. We shall return to these findings after presenting our econometric results for short-run shifting.

# CHAPTER 3

# GENERAL METHOD, SOURCES, AND VARIABLES

## A. GENERAL METHOD

THE CONCLUSION OF THE preceding chapter is that little can be said unless a way is found to isolate the tax effect. This task is limited by the fact that the period for which pertinent data are available is rather short and includes two subperiods, the Great Depression and World War II, which have to be excluded due to unusual conditions. At the same time, the analysis is complex and requires that the effects of many non-tax factors be eliminated.

To gain points of observation, these limitations suggest the use of firm data, so as to permit combination of time and cross-section analysis. This was our original intent, but it turned out that the tax variable does not differ sufficiently between firms to permit cross-section analysis.[1] Next, we experimented with combining time and cross-section analysis for non-tax variables, with time analysis used for tax variables only. The complication, however, did not prove worth the improvement in results. We thus arrived at a time analysis with one of the indicators as the dependent variable, and tax factors appearing among the pre-determined variables.

The next step was to choose between the share and the rate-of-return approach. Various considerations led us to prefer the latter. While both indicators are significant, the rate-of-return approach is of more immediate importance from an incentive (growth effects) as well as equity (bearing on the "double taxation" issue) point of view. It is conceptually simpler and more feasible in terms of available data. This is the case especially once one disects the over-all picture. One of the interesting applications of this type of analysis should be to test hypotheses about differential degrees of shifting in various subgroups, depending upon size, type of industry, market position,

---

[1] This is obviously the case for statutory rates of tax, but it is also the case for effective rates, and for a definition of the tax variable (see model A below) as the ratio of tax liability to capital.

etc. Since data on value added is not readily available by subgroups, there was good reason to expect that in dealing with industrial subgroups a rate-of-return approach would be more feasible than a share approach.

Two further issues could be resolved on purely pragmatic grounds. Available data do not suffice to measure long-run effects, nor do they permit inclusion of unincorporated business. We thus arrive at indicators 5 and 6 of Table 2–1, measuring short-run effects of the corporation tax on the rate of return on corporate capital. It seemed desirable, moreover, to limit our broadest group to all manufacturing corporations rather than all corporations, since this leaves us with a more homogenous body of data. As it turned out, the thrust of our findings relates largely to the all-manufacturing group as a whole, but some subgroups are considered as well.

## B. DATA AND COVERAGE

*Coverage in Time*

The major part of our analysis makes use of industry data from the U.S. Treasury's *Statistics of Income,* beginning in 1935 and extending to 1959.[2] Inclusion of the early thirties would have been undesirable, and comparable data for the twenties are not readily available. In addition, we use data for samples of individual companies or for individual companies drawn from *Moody's Manual of Investments,* beginning 1936 and extending to 1959. Loss of the first year was unavoidable for the company data, since figures on capital are needed with a one period lag and *Moody's* data is less satisfactory prior to 1935, this being the year when SEC reporting begins. In both cases, the years from 1943 to 1947 are excluded, since price controls and heavy government purchases created altogether unusual conditions.

*Industry Groups and Samples*

The data from *Statistics of Income* include the all-manufacturing group and various industry groups. The particular groups were chosen because they involve the least change in composition of data over the period covered, and thus required a minimum of adjustment:

[2] For a more detailed description of sources and basic data for the all-manufacturing case see p. 67.

All manufacturing
All manufacturing with assets over $50 million
All manufacturing with assets under $50 million
Leather
Rubber
Paper
Food
Stone

All returns, taxable and non-taxable, are included. Exclusion of non-taxable returns might have improved the relation between the tax and rate-of-return variables, but would have reduced the homogeneity of the data.

The data from *Moody's* include two industry samples and two other groups:

Steel (26 companies)
Textiles (12 companies)
15 largest companies (price leaders)
15 largest companies (price followers)

With regard to steel companies, a larger number of firms was available and a random choice was made. The textile companies were chosen so as to exclude all companies which changed identity through merger or splits, persistent loss companies, or companies with inadequate coverage. A further sample was made of the 30 largest manufacturing companies, which were then divided into the 15 most likely to act as price leaders, and the 15 most likely to act as price followers.[3] The general picture presented by these samples is included in Tables 2-6 and 2-7. Finally General Motors and U.S. Steel are analyzed as individual firms.

### Adjustments of Data

The data from *Statistics of Income* could be used essentially in its reported form, while the data from *Moody's* had to be corrected in a more detailed way to allow for differences in reporting, and for peculiarities arising in connection with individual firms.[4] In addition to using the data in this form, we also undertook to adjust the all-manufacturing series for inflation and for accelerated depreciation.

*Inflation.* There has been widespread complaint that the postwar profit picture has been distorted by failure to allow for depreciation allowances

[3] For list of companies, see below, p. 72.
[4] See p. 68.

sufficient to cover rising replacement cost. Moreover, the inflation occurred over years during which tax rates rose. This poses the question of whether the evidence on shifting remains the same if the inflation factor is adjusted for.

A correction for inflation was made and includes an adjustment in capital as well as in profits. Inventory valuation profits are disallowed. The adjustment is based on the construction of two indices, showing for an imaginary company the ratio of capital and depreciation under replacement cost depreciation to capital and depreciation under historical cost depreciation. The investment behavior of the imaginary company is assumed to equal that of the economy as a whole (beginning with 1913) and straight line depreciation over 15 years is assumed.[5]

*Depreciation.* In dealing with taxation effects on the rate of return on capital, a distinction may be drawn between effects which result from changes in depreciation schedules, and those which stem from changes in tax rates. Since the two are related over time, there is the possibility that the tax-variable coefficient will reflect effects of changing depreciation policies. An attempt is made to examine this for all-manufacturing.[6]

## C. KEY VARIABLES

The essence of our analysis is to fit a function with the tax factors among the variables which determine the rate of return. Before turning to the details of the model, we consider the definition of these key variables.

### Tax Variables

*Form of Tax Function.* In constructing the model, the dependent variable must be related to the independent variables, including the tax variable. This variable and the form of its functional relationship must be decided upon prior to estimating its coefficients. Since the correct choice is not known a priori, the formulation used can be evaluated only *ex post*. It is well to begin with simple linear formulations such as:

$$(3\text{–}A) \qquad\qquad Y_g - Y' = a\frac{T}{K}$$

[5] See p. 77.
[6] See p. 53.

where the period of adjustment is too short to permit a tax induced change in the capital stock $K$ during the period.

Another formulation is:

(3–B) $$Y_g - Y' = bZ.$$

The behavioral assumption implied in (3–A) is that the firm adjusts itself so as to increase the gross rate of return sufficiently to recoup a given fraction $a$ of the negative rate of return (defined as the ratio of tax liability $T$ to capital) suffered from the tax.[7] The behavioral assumption implied in (3–B) is that the firm raises its rate of return by a constant fraction of the tax rate.[8]

Further multiplying by $K$, the formulas become:

(3–A*) $$\pi_g - \pi' = aT$$

and

(3–B*) $$\pi_g - \pi' = \frac{b}{Y_g}T.$$

According to (3–A*) the firm raises its profits by a constant fraction of its tax liability, independently of the level of profits or the level of tax. According to (3–B*) the increase in profits as a fraction of the tax varies inversely with

---

[7] Under certain definitions of measure of shifting, as given on p. 39, it happens that $a$ also becomes a measure of the degree of shifting. Our immediate concern in equation 3–A, however, is with business behavior regarding shifting and not its measurement.

[8] In search for other simple behavior assumptions one might assume the firm to focus on its net rate of return and write:

$$Y' - Y_n = A\frac{T}{K}$$

where the firm permits its net rate to fall by a given fraction of the negative rate of return imposed by the tax. This, however, is perfectly equivalent to (3–A) in the text since

$$Y' - Y_n = (1 - a)\frac{T}{K}$$

thus, preserving the same linear $\left(\text{in } \frac{T}{K}\right)$ form, the constant coefficient $A$ being the complement to $a$.

Taking the net view of the $B$ formulation, we may write:

$$Y' - Y_n = BZ$$

where the firm permits its net rate of return to be reduced by a given fraction of the rate of tax. This is not equivalent to (3–B) in the text. It involves a different though perhaps as reasonable behavior assumption. Since $Y_n = (1 - Z)Y_g$, the new behavior assumption may be written in gross terms as

$$Y' - (1 - Z)Y_g = BZ$$

which is non-linear in $Z$. Where as the gross and net approach are equivalent for the $A$ approach, they differ for the $B$ approach. The gross approach was chosen, but brief attention is given to the net approach as well. See p. 88.

the rate of return, thus running counter to the view that shifting will tend to be larger in a seller's market. Since $Y_g$ is related positively to the tax rate if shifting occurs, the measure also implies that the fraction shifted is related inversely to the tax rate. This runs counter to the hypothesis of restrained monopoly pricing. On economic grounds, the hypothesis underlying (3–A) seems preferable, but both will be tested.

Two additional properties of (3–A) and (3–B) may be noted. Equation (3–B) may be rewritten as $Y_g - Y' = bZ$ which is linear in $Z$. Since $T = Z\pi_g$, equation (3–A) similarly rewritten becomes $Y_g - Y' = aZY_g$ which is non-linear in $Z$.[9] This complicates statistical formulation and estimation if behavior assumption $A$ is used. Relation $B$ is linear in $Z$ and can be estimated readily by least squares. Nevertheless, the behavior assumption underlying model A seems more sensible and we shall find that model A is statistically superior.

*Statutory vs. Effective Rate.* In the (3–A) formulation, the tax variable enters as absolute liabilities. In the formulation of (3–B) where the tax rate $Z$ is used, we must choose between interpreting $Z$ as the statutory rate or the effective rate. The effective rates (ratio of tax liability to profits before tax) for all-manufacturing corporations are shown in Col. V of Table 3–1, while the statutory rates are shown in Cols. II to IV. The statutory rate is defined as the rate applicable to larger corporations, which supply the bulk of the yield and dominate the aggregate picture. As may be expected, the effective rate usually falls below the statutory rate, due to loss companies, progression, and other factors. Both rates are used for the B formulation.[10]

*Single vs. Combined Rates.* In defining the tax variable, a decision must be made for either behavioral assumption, whether to combine the corporation profits and excess profits taxes, or whether to treat them separately. In favor of separate treatment is the presumption that the reaction of businessmen to the two taxes may differ. The excess profits tax is less permanent, and typically applies under unusual conditions. In favor of combined treatment is the fact that the two tax rates are correlated, and that a degree of freedom is gained by estimating one instead of two regression coefficients. Attempts at separate treatment resulted in greatly increased error terms for the regression coefficients, so that combined treatment was preferable.

*Differential Rate.* Since the corporation tax is partial in that it applies to the corporate sector only, it is of interest to consider the effects of the differential between the rates applicable to investment in the corporate and

---

[9] Note that *this* non-linearity results from the dependence of $T$ on $Y$, and has nothing to do with the non-linearity issues discussed in the preceding note.

[10] See Table 6–3, p. 50.

Table 3–1. Tax Rates

| Income year | Corporation taxes | | | | | Combined corporate and individual marginal tax rate on equity income paid by average shareholder[c] | Individual marginal tax rate on dividend income paid by average shareholder[d] | Differential rate [VII-VIII] |
| | Marginal statutory rates | | | Ratio of tax liability[b] to | | | | |
| | Profits tax | Excess profits tax[a] | Total[a] | Profits (effective rate) | Net worth | | | |
| I | II | III | IV | V | VI | VII | VIII | IX |
|---|---|---|---|---|---|---|---|---|
| 1929 | .11 | — | .11 | .138967* | .016252* | n.c. | n.c. | n.c. |
| 1934 | .1375 | — | .1375 | .265925 | .006893 | n.c. | .241454 | n.c. |
| 1935 | .1375 | — | .1375 | .193777 | .009305 | .290933 | .241454 | .049479 |
| 1936 | .15 | — | .15 | .164245 | .015608 | .353992 | .264298 | .089694 |
| 1937 | .15 | — | .15 | .174707 | .016664 | .346078 | .264298 | .081780 |
| 1938 | .19 | — | .19 | .232354 | .009020 | .361787 | .264298 | .097489 |
| 1939 | .19 | — | .19 | .176735 | .015245 | .340328 | .264298 | .076030 |
| 1940 | .24 | — | .24 | .291210 | .036383 | .367437 | .262250 | .105187 |
| 1941 | .31 | .30 | .61 | .473883 | .110520 | .687809 | .362167 | .325642 |
| 1942 | .40 | .40 | .80 | .602333 | .168564 | .785915 | .446425 | .339490 |
| 1943 | .40 | .40 | .80 | .635355 | .189388 | n.c. | n.c. | n.c. |
| 1944 | .40 | .40 | .80 | .632157 | .153539 | .858847 | .514284 | .344563 |
| 1945 | .40 | .40 | .80 | .596087 | .096147 | .870273 | .514284 | .355989 |
| 1946 | .38 | — | .38 | .395009 | .070817 | .546284 | .540114 | .006170 |
| 1947 | .38 | — | .38 | .378862 | .092338 | .533547 | .540114 | —.006567 |
| 1948 | .38 | — | .38 | .375952 | .088164 | .515455 | .440042 | .075413 |
| 1949 | .38 | — | .38 | .384767 | .064769 | .536956 | .440042 | .096914 |
| 1950 | .42 | — | .42 | .448017 | .118974 | .562615 | .440042 | .122573 |
| 1951 | .5075 | .17 | .6775 | .569392 | .144887 | .779422 | .512033 | .267389 |
| 1952 | .52 | .18 | .70 | .561143 | .108360 | .808709 | .512033 | .296676 |
| 1953 | .52 | .18 | .70 | .566367 | .110086 | .804353 | .512033 | .292320 |
| 1954 | .52 | — | .52 | .516113 | .082460 | .689086 | .515514 | .173572 |
| 1955 | .52 | — | .52 | .499612 | .108097 | .689086 | .515514 | .173572 |
| 1956 | .52 | — | .52 | .498570 | .093204 | .689086 | .515514 | .173572 |
| 1957 | .52 | — | .52 | .506820 | .082604 | .695162 | .515514 | .179648 |
| 1958 | .52 | — | .52 | .509619 | .064105 | .692136 | .515514 | .176622 |
| 1959 | .52 | — | .52 | .497678 | .080291 | .692136 | .515514 | .176622 |

See page 29 for footnotes.

in the unincorporated sector. Indeed, it is this differential rather than the absolute rate which matters if emphasis is placed on induced capital flows between the two sectors.[11] For this purpose, we computed the "total" tax on operating profits paid by the investor in a corporation. This tax includes the corporation tax on the entire profits; the marginal individual income tax rate on such part of net profits as is dividend income; and a capital gains rate on that part of retained earnings as is assumed to be realized by sale. This "total" tax (shown in Col. VII of Table 3–1) is compared with the marginal rate (shown in Col. VIII) paid by an individual investor on the operating profits of his unincorporated investment, it being assumed that such income is distributed like dividend income. The differential between the two is given in Col. IX. The significance of the differential rate approach will be considered further when the results are examined.[12]

*Timing.* Consideration must be given to the timing of the tax effect. Our model clearly cannot measure the "long-run" effects in the traditional sense of taxation effects on and through changes in the stock of capital. While working capital may be adjusted quickly, it may be assumed that effects on plant and equipment take a considerable time to appear. Although our analysis covers up to 20 years, the number of observations do not suffice to introduce a time lag in the tax variable sufficient to measure the longer run effects over, say, 10 years. The data is sufficient to accommodate a tax variable with a time lag of a few years, but it appeared that the significance of the tax variable drops off sharply after the year of change in tax. Thus only the current-period tax variable is included.[13] This, to be sure, does not mean that the measured effect occurred altogether in the year of change since tax changes

[11] See p. 5.
[12] See p. 57.
[13] See p. 44.

---

Footnotes for Table 3–1.

[a] For 1941–45, the total rate shown is the maximum rate, and the excess profits rate is defined as the difference between the maximum and the corporation tax rate.

[b] Includes corporation profits tax, excess profits tax, and undistributed profits tax in *all manufacturing*, loss companies included. The undistributed profits tax is disregarded in col. II and IV.

[c] Computed as follows:

Let $q_t$ = ratio of all dividends paid to total profits after taxes in year $t$ for all manufacturing
$X_t$ = capital gains rate in year $t$
$Z_t$ = total marginal statutory corporate rate (column IV)
$U_t$ = individual marginal rate (column VIII)
$V_t$ = corporate and individual rate on equity income (column VII)
Then

$$V_t = Z_t + q_t(1 - Z_t)U_t + .2(1 - Z_t).X_t$$

The value of .2 is the assumed fraction of capital gains which are realized.

[d] Computed for any one year by applying marginal individual income tax rates to dividend incomes by brackets, aggregating tax thus computed for all income brackets and dividing by total dividend income. The computation was not made for each year, the computed marginal rate being assumed constant over certain years when tax rates did not change. This assumes that dividend distribution remained constant over these years.
* Estimated

in successive years are correlated.  However, the major part of the measured effect must have come about rapidly, i.e., in one or a few years' span.  That is to say, our analysis relates to what traditionally has been referred to as the "short-run" effect, i.e., adjustments which operate through price, wage, or output changes, with a given capital stock.  These changes come about rapidly but their consequences may remain present for a long time.  As noted before, our concept of "short-run" shifting relates to speed of adjustment, so that we may talk about the long-run implications of short-run effects.[14]


### Rate of Return

*Gross vs. Net Rate.*  In defining the dependent variable in our system, a choice must be made between the use of the gross rate $Y_g$ and the net rate $Y_n$. Using the behavioral assumption (3–A), the choice is a matter of indifference. This is not so for behavioral assumption (3–B).  If stated in gross terms in linear form, it is non-linear in net terms and vice versa.[15]  We adopt the gross formulation for model B and, to be consistent, formulate model A in gross terms as well.

*Equity vs. Total Capital.*  We now turn to a second choice, which is between the rate of return on equity capital and the rate of return on total capital. In the one case we use the ratio of profits to equity capital; in the other, we use the ratio of profits plus interest paid to total capital, where total capital equals equity capital plus all (short and long) interest bearing debt.

Since the corporation tax applies to profits only, there may be a presumption in favor of using the profit to equity ratio.  But the tax may induce substitution of debt for equity finance, thus raising the ratio of gross profit to equity.  This would result in a higher measure of shifting than would apply without change in financial structure.  The result, as noted before, would be misleading because the implications of such an increase in the ratio of profit to equity are quite different from those of shifting by price increase. Moreover, the resulting increase in the return on equity may be deceptive because it is offset by an increase in the shareholder's risk.  If the rate of return on total capital is used, this difficulty is largely avoided.

More basically, it may be argued that one should use that formulation which is most relevant to business behavior, and which yields the superior fit of the rate of return function.  Both approaches were tried, and we find that there is little difference.

[14] See p. 2.
[15] See note 8, p. 26.

*Risk Rate.* The hypothesis may be advanced that shifting should be related to the excess of profit income over the bond rate, i.e., to the return on risk taking. For this purpose, a gross rate of risk return (i.e., that part of the gross rate of return, before deducting tax, which is imputable to risk) for all-manufacturing was computed by deducting the yield on triple A corporate bonds from the gross rate of return.

## Other Variables

The rate of return, of course, cannot be explained by the tax factor only, and other predetermined variables are needed. Use is made of the change in consumption, expenditures lagged one year, the inventory to sales ratio for all manufacturing lagged one year, and of other tax rates defined as the ratio of yield from other taxes to GNP. Additional variables, especially government expenditures, were experimented with and will be noted later.[16]

[16] See p. 47.

# CHAPTER 4

# THE MODELS

AS NOTED BEFORE, our general approach is to apply time analysis to fit a function where the rate of return is the dependent variable, and tax factors are among the predetermined variables. This permits us to determine the regression coefficients of the tax variables, and on this basis to estimate the difference between the observed rate of return and what the rate of return would have been without tax. From this a measure of shifting is derived.

## Definitions and Notations

The following definitions and notations are used in this and later chapters:

$\pi_{g,t}$    gross profits, equal to profits before tax, for equity base; gross profits plus interest paid, for total capital base.

$\pi_{n,t}$    net profits, equal to profits after tax, for equity base; net profits plus interest paid, for total capital base.

$K_t$    net worth, for equity base; net worth plus interest bearing debt, for total capital base.

$Y_{g,t}$    gross rate of return, defined as

$$Y_{g,t} = \frac{\pi_{g,t}}{K_{t-1}}.$$

$Y_{n,t}$    net rate of return, defined as

$$Y_{n,t} = \frac{\pi_{n,t}}{K_{t-1}}.$$

$Y'$    priming of $Y$ variables indicates their estimated value for zero tax.

$X_t$    general notation for tax variable.

$T_t$    tax liability, accrual base.

$L_t$    standardized tax liability, defined as

$$L_t = \frac{T_t}{K_{t-1}}.$$

$Z_t$    statutory tax rate (see Table 3-1).
$Z_t^*$    effective tax rate, defined as

$$Z_t^* = \frac{T_t}{\pi_{g,t}}.$$

$Z_t^{**}$    differential tax rate, (see Table 3-1).
$L_t^{**}$    ratio of differential tax liability to capital, defined as

$$L_t^{**} = \frac{Z_t^{**}}{Z_t^*} L_t.$$

$C_t$    consumption expenditure standardized by division by GNP.
$V_t$    ratio of inventory to sales in manufacturing.
$J_t$    ratio of tax accruals (all levels of government) other than corporate tax, minus government transfers, to GNP.
$G_t$    Federal purchases, standardized by division by GNP.
$E_t$    Moody's Aaa rate on bonds.
$B_t$    surplus $(+)$ or deficit $(-)$ in Federal Budget, standardized by division by GNP.
$U_t$    stochastic variable.
$S$    measure of shifting.
$F_t$    ratio of profits to value added.

## Rate of Return Function

We wish to determine a function which permits us to predict changes in the gross rate of return $Y_g$ which result from changes in tax rates. This function should be the reduced form in $Y_g$ of a general system involving the tax factor as one of the determinants of $Y_g$. While it is not our purpose here to develop a general macro system, such a general system, more or less in line with our formulation, is given in a note at the end of this chapter.

Having only a limited number of observations, the number of predetermined variables had to be severly restricted. In order to obtain an adequate explanation of $Y_g$, variables had to be looked for which are highly correlated with $Y_g$, but not with each other. Experimentation led to the following formulation:

$$(4) \quad Y_{g,t} = a_0 + a_1 \Delta C_{t-1} + a_2 V_{t-1} + a_3 J_t + a_4 X_t + a_5 G_t + a_6 X_{t-1} + U_t$$

where $\Delta C$ is the change in consumption, $V$ is the inventory to sales ratio for all manufacturing, $J$ is the tax variable for taxes other than corporation tax, $G$ is Federal purchases, and $X$ is the corporate tax variable, to be defined more specifically later. Use was made of lagged variables to obtain a better determination of the system.

*Model B*

In equation (4) the tax factor was written in general form. It must now be made more specific. As shown in Chapter 3, two behavioral assumptions may be used. Beginning with that stated in (3–B), use is made of the tax rate whether as statutory rate $Z$ or as effective rate $Z^*$. Our model becomes

(4B)  $Y_{g,t} = b_0 + b_1 C_{t-1} + b_2 V_{t-1} + b_3 J_t + b_4 Z_t + b_5 G_t + b_6 Z_{t-1} + U_t.$

This model is fully reduced and may be readily estimated by least squares,[1] using either $Z$ or $Z^*$.

*Model A*

Alternatively, we may follow the behavioral assumption of (3–A). The tax variable here takes the form of tax liability $T$, where $T = Z\pi_g$. In this case the tax variable is not independent and the system is not fully reduced. Nevertheless, it is desirable to estimate the tax effect in this form, because, as shown above, businessmen may well think of shifting as recovering a given tax liability. The $T$ variable is standardized by division by $K_{-1}$, where $L = T/K_{-1}$. Our model then becomes

(4–A)  $Y_{g,t} = a_0 + a_1 C_{t-1} + a_2 V_{t-1} + a_3 J_t + a_4 L_t + a_5 G_t + a_6 L_{t-1} + U_t.$

Since $L_t$ is a dependent variable, the least squares method is liable to give inconsistent results. After considerable experimentation, it seemed best to resolve the estimating problem for this model by the instrumental-variable approach.[2]

The nature of the instrumental-variable approach need not be discussed here,[3] and a brief description of the estimating procedure is given below.[4] It should be noted, however, that we are less subject to the usual objection of arbitrariness in the choice of instrument since $Z^*$ is the obvious instrument

$$L_t = T/K_{t-1} = Z_t^* Y_{g,t}.$$

for $L$. As may be expected, it proves to be highly correlated with $L_t$.

---

[1] For prerequisite specifications, see p. 94.

[2] Klein's approximation procedure (Lawrence R. Klein, *A Textbook of Econometrics*, [Evanston, Ill.: Row, Peterson & Co., 1953] pp. 120–21) gives very similar results, see p. 98.

[3] See Stefan Valavanis, *Econometrics*, (New York: McGraw-Hill Book Co., 1959), pp. 107–25. L. R. Klein, *op. cit.*, pp. 122–25, and J. D. Sargan, "The Estimation of Economic Relationships Using Instrumental Variables," *Econometrica*, vol. 25, no. 3, July, 1958, pp. 393–415.

[4] See p. 98.

## Differencing

The models were experimented with in both differenced and undifferenced form. Since there is usually no positive serial auto-correlation in our errors of prediction,[5] the undifferenced form is preferable.

## Note on General Model

As noted before, it cannot be our purpose here to develop a general macro model, but the type of system underlying equation (4) above may be sketched. The terms used, which in some cases differ from those in the text, are as follows:

$Q$     quantity of output
$N$     labor input
$N^*$   labor force
$C$     consumption expenditure, money terms
$I$      investment expenditure, money terms
$G$     government expenditures
$w_g$    money wage rate
$J$      personal tax rate
$\pi_g$     gross profits
$Z$     profits tax rate
$V_{-1}$   ratio of inventory to sales
$M$    potential money supply, defined as excess reserves weighted by reciprocal reserve ratios
$K_{-1}$   capital stock at beginning of the period
$Y_g$    gross rate of return.

The general model takes this form:

## Functions

| | | |
|---|---|---|
| Production | $Q$ | $= Q[N, K_{-1}]$ |
| Aggregate demand | $QP$ | $= C + I + G$ |
| Consumption | $C$ | $= C[w_g(1 - J)N, \pi_g(1 - Z), M, K_{-1}, P]$ |
| Investment | $I$ | $= I[Y_g, Z, \Delta C_{-1}, G, V_{-1}, M, K_{-1}, P, w_g]$ |
| Labor supply | $N$ | $= N_s[w_g, J, P, N^*]$ |
| Labor demand | $N$ | $= N_d[w_g, P, K_{-1}]$ |
| Prices | $P$ | $= P[M, w_g, J, Z, Q, C]$ |
| Definition | $Y_g$ | $= \dfrac{\pi_g}{K_{-1}}$ |

[5] Without differencing the Durbin-Watson statistics usually exceeded 2 and after differencing showed still higher values.

The model has been written in a sufficiently general form to avoid any dogmatism regarding the choice between Keynesian vs. neo-classical or competitive vs. imperfectly competitive systems.

The predetermined variables are $K_{-1}$, $G$, $M$, $J$, $N^*$, $\Delta C_{-1}$, $V_{-1}$, $Z$, while the other eight, $Q$, $N$, $P$, $C$, $I$, $w_g$, $\pi_g$ and $Y_g$, are determined by the system. A reduced form of $Y_g$ might then be given by

$$Y_g = Y_g(K_{-1},\ G,\ M,\ J,\ N^*,\ \Delta C_{-1},\ V_{-1},\ Z)$$

which, however, would be a very complex relationship and not amenable to estimation in this connection. Since $Y_g$ is a ratio, variables with absolute dimensions must be standardized if the relation is to be written in linear form. We then obtain

$$Y_g = a_0 + a_1\Delta\left(\frac{C}{GNP}\right)_{-1} + a_2V_{-1} + a_3J + a_4\left(\frac{G}{GNP}\right) + a_5Z + u$$

with $\Delta C$ and $G$ being standardized by division by $GNP$. The $N^*$ variable was dropped as it proved wholly unrelated to $Y_g$. The addition of the $M$ variable resulted in a slight reduction in $R$ adjusted for degrees of freedom and was dropped. The $K_{-1}$ variable is dropped as well since it proved collinear with other variables. Use of $K_{-1}$ in place of $GNP$ as the standardizing variable for $\Delta C_{-1}$ and $G_t$ did not alter the results significantly.

Equation (4) in the text is in line with this equation (note the symbols $C$ and $G$ as there used allow for standardizing) except for these differences: (1) the tax rate $J$ is extended to include all taxes other than corporation profits tax; (2) government expenditures are restricted to Federal purchases; (3) the tax variable is written in more general form, subject to later specification.

The general model, given in this note, relates to the entire economy. It could readily be expanded to allow for a corporate and a non-corporate sector, each subject to different rates of tax. The dependent variable could then be related to either sector or to both sectors combined, as would be suggested by Harberger's analysis.[6] Retaining $Y_g$ for the corporate sector as the dependent variable in the two sector approach, however, would double the number of explanatory variables and for this our degrees of freedom are insufficient. Nor can we combine both sectors and consider the net return on total capital, because the data for the unincorporated sectors are inadequate. In order to take some cognizance of this problem, we experiment with introducing a differential rate, defined as the difference between the rates of tax applicable in the two sectors, as an additional variable; but for the bulk of our analysis equation 4 is used.

[6] See p. 4, note 3, and p. 57.

# CHAPTER 5

# DEGREES OF SHIFTING IN THE ESTIMATED MODELS

THE MODELS DEVELOPED in the preceding chapter will permit us to estimate the regression coefficients (slopes) of tax variables. It remains to translate these coefficients into a measure of the degree of shifting.

*Measures of Shifting*

In Table 2–2 we showed the conditions for zero and 100 per cent shifting under the rate of return indicator. We must now go further and determine how to measure the precise degree of shifting, if it is not zero or 100 per cent.

We have seen that under the rate of return indicator there is only one meaningful way of defining zero and 100 per cent shifting. The conditions for the rate of return indicator may be written in either gross terms,

zero shifting $\qquad\qquad\qquad\qquad\qquad Y_{g,t} = Y'$

100 per cent shifting $\qquad\qquad Y_{g,t} - Y' = Z_t^* Y_{g,t}$

or in net terms

zero shifting $\qquad\qquad\qquad\qquad\qquad Y_{g,t} = Y'$

100 per cent shifting $\qquad (1 - Z_t^*)Y_{g,t} - (1 - Z_t^*)Y' = Z_t^* Y'$

As shown before, the two formulations are equivalent.

When it comes to measuring degrees of shifting other than zero and 100 per cent, many measures may be defined, all of which satisfy the above conditions for zero and 100 per cent shifting but show different degrees of shifting at other values. The gross formulation above suggests a measure of shifting

$$(5\text{–}1) \qquad\qquad S_t = \frac{Y_{g,t} - Y'}{Z_t^* Y_{g,t}}$$

while the net formulation suggests

$$(5\text{–}2) \qquad\qquad S_t^* = \frac{(1 - Z_t^*)Y_{g,t} - (1 - Z_t^*)Y'}{Z_t^* Y'}.$$

The two measures are again interchangeable for zero and 100 per cent shifting, but they differ for other values.

The economic significance of $S_t$ is that it measures the ratio of gross gain from raising the gross rate of return, to actual tax paid. The economic meaning of $S_t^*$ is that it measures the ratio of net gain from raising the gross rate of return, to the loss from the tax had there been no adjustment. In a sense, the first measure gives the fraction of actual loss recouped, while the second gives the fraction of potential loss avoided.

The two measures may be compared most easily in absolute profit terms, which, for the short-run case, is equivalent to the rate of return formulation. We then have

$$S_t = \frac{\pi_{g,t} - \pi'}{Z_t^* \pi_{g,t}} \quad \text{and} \quad S_t^* = \frac{(1 - Z_t^*)\pi_{g,t} - (1 - Z_t^*)\pi'}{Z_t^* \pi'}.$$

Graphically, this may be presented as follows:

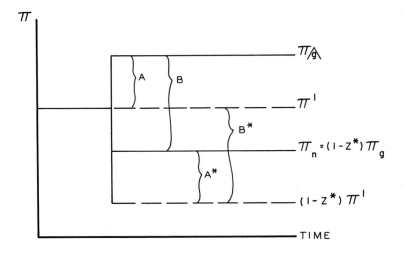

where $S_t = \dfrac{A}{B}$ and $S_t^* = \dfrac{A^*}{B^*}$. Both concepts are meaningful, but there are various reasons for preferring $S$.

The measure $S$ fits nicely into the traditional way of dividing the tax between the part born by the consumer and that born by the firm, since it expresses the degree of shifting as the ratio of the consumer's part to the total tax.[1] This also appears to be the measure that is relevant for the discussion of "integration" of the corporation with the individual income tax, under conditions where the corporation tax is partly shifted.

The *S* measure will be used in interpreting our econometric analysis and was also the concept applied in measuring degrees of shifting (for the rate of return indicator) in Chapter 2.[2] Further exploration of the *S\** measure is relegated to the appendix.[3]

Having clarified the substantive difference between $S_t$ and $S_t^*$, it remains to be noted that either may be estimated from a $Y_g$ or $Y_n$ function. Formulations (5–1) and (5–2) were both written in gross terms, because $Y_g$ rather than $Y_n$ is the dependent variable in our econometric model.[4] These formulations will henceforth be referred to as $S_{g,t}$ and $S_{g,t}^*$.

*Introduction of Shifting Measure into Model A*

We begin with model A and assume that the tax variable appears in an unlagged form only. Using equation (4–A), we estimate $Y_t'$ by setting $L_t = 0$. That is to say, we estimate what the rate of return in any one year would have been had the tax rate been zero, the other variables for that year being independent of the tax. Consequently $Y_{g,t} - Y_t' = a_4 L_t$. Rewriting the measure of $S_{g,t}$ defined in equation (5–1) as

$$S_{g,t} = \frac{Y_{g,t} - Y_t'}{L_t}$$

we get (5–3A)

$$S_{g,t} = a_4.$$

In the case of model A, the shifting measure in its gross formulation thus happily coincides with the estimated coefficient of the tax variable.[5] The shifting measure is a constant over time. Moreover, the relation involved in the shifting measure is the same as that involved in the tax variable in the rate-of-return function. The shifting measure is thus independent of the level of tax and of the rate of return.

---

[1] We have $T_t = [\pi' - \pi_{g,t}(1 - Z^*)] + [\pi_{g,t} - \pi']$ where the first term on the right is the company's share, and the second term is the consumer's share. See Dalton, *op. cit.*, p. 73.

[2] We now consider shifting of the total tax, not as in Chapter 2, the addition to an initial tax. See p. 14, note 10.

[3] See p. 83.

[4] See p. 30.

[5] See note 7, p. 26.

Allowing now for both lagged and unlagged tax variables, and setting both equal to zero, we obtain $Y_{g,t} - Y'_t = a_4L_t + a_6L_{t-1}$. Thus the measure becomes

$$(5\text{-}4\text{A}) \qquad\qquad S_{g,t} = a_4 + a_6 \frac{L_{t-1}}{L_t}.$$

The weight of $a_6$ in the shifting measure depends positively on the change in tax liability, reflecting the lagged nature of the tax variable involved. Because of the differing weight of $a_6$, the value of $S$ may now vary from year to year.

This complication is avoided if, to obtain a bird's eye view, we compute $S$ for the average value of the tax variables. We then obtain

$$(5\text{-}5\text{A}) \qquad\qquad S_{g.} = a_4 + a_6 \frac{(L.)_{-1}}{L.}$$

for the combined degree of shifting where . in subscript indicates average of the variable.

*Introduction of Shifting Measure into Model B*

We now turn to model B, beginning again with the unlagged tax variable. Using equation (4–B) we estimate $Y'_t$ by setting $Z_t = 0$. We obtain $Y_{g,t} - Y'_t = b_4Z_t$. Substituting into our measure of $S_{g,t}$ we get

$$(5\text{-}3\text{B}) \qquad\qquad S_{g,t} = \frac{b_4}{Y_{g,t}}.$$

The measure of shifting now depends inversely on the rate of return. If the gross rate of return rises with the tax due to shifting while holding other factors constant, the measured degree of shifting declines with the rate of tax. This reflects the behavior assumption (3–B) according to which the slope of the relationship between tax rate and rate of return is constant, but the fraction of tax recovered in higher profits varies with $Y_{g,t}$ and $Z_t$.

Allowing for both lagged and unlagged tax variables and setting both equal to zero we obtain $Y_{g,t} - Y'_t = b_4Z_t + b_6Z_{t-1}$. Thus we obtain

$$(5\text{-}4\text{B}) \qquad\qquad S_{g,t} = \frac{b_4}{Y_{g,t}} + \frac{b_6}{Y_{g,t}} \frac{(Z_t)_{-1}}{Z_t}$$

for the combined degree of shifting.

*Behavior Rules vs. Shifting Concepts*

In the preceding pages we have dealt with two substantive problems. The one was the choice of hypotheses describing the behavior of firms with regard to shifting, and leading to models A and B. These behavior hypotheses, implied in the form in which the tax variable is related to the rate of return, describe the general way in which the firm reacts to a change in tax rate. The second and entirely different problem was to define a measure of shifting. Having decided in favor of definition $S$ as against $S^*$, $S$ was then introduced into both models.

The question arises whether the behavior assumptions (i.e., the appropriate way of introducing the tax factor) should not have been defined to begin with in terms of the shifting measure, so that the coefficient of the tax factor directly records the degree of shifting. The answer is no, because different considerations apply. The shifting measure must be chosen so as to evaluate the results of the tax in a way which points up socially significant implications. The behavior rule, as expressed by the form of the function must be chosen so as to describe the actual behavior of the firm, and the merit of the rule can be tested by the goodness of the fit. In the case of model A, the regression coefficient for the unlagged tax variable happens to coincide with $S$, but this coincidence would disappear if $S^*$ were used. In the case of model B, the regression coefficient differs with either formulation of the degree of shifting, and thus must be translated into $S$ or $S^*$.

While there is no need for the regression coefficient and the measure of shifting to coincide, it is convenient if they do. The degree of shifting will then be a constant for all levels of tax rate or rate of return, simply because the regression coefficient is a constant. If they differ, the degree of shifting (as estimated by the particular shifting measure) will depend on these variables.[6] We were happy to find, therefore, that model A for which $S = a_4$ gave the better fit, and that $S$ seemed more significant from a policy point of view than $S^*$.

---

[6] See p. 87.

# CHAPTER 6

# BASIC RESULTS FOR ALL-MANUFACTURING, TOTAL CAPITAL BASE

WE NOW TURN to the estimates, beginning in this chapter with the case of All-Manufacturing, total capital base. The results are given in Tables 6–1 and 6–3. The core of our finding lies in the standard case of Table 6–1, line 3 and will not be altered greatly by the additional cases to be examined in the next chapter.

## A. MODEL A

*Main Results*

Model A was estimated first on the basis of equation (4–A), the results being given in line 1 of Table 6–1. The value of $R$ is high at .98. The unlagged tax variable shows 145 per cent shifting and is highly significant at the 1 per cent level.[1] The lagged tax variable shows slight shifting but is not significant. The negative sign of the coefficient for the $G$ variable is surprising, but the coefficient is not significant.

The simple correlation matrix given in Table 6–2 shows that one of the two least significant variables, $L_{t-1}$, is highly correlated with $Z_t$ the instrument for $L_t$. This suggests that the model be tried without $L_{t-1}$. As shown in line 2 of Table 6–1, elimination of $L_{t-1}$ increases the significance of most other coefficients. The least significant coefficient is now $G_t$. As shown in line 3, further elimination of $G_t$ increases the significance of all coefficients. The coefficient of the unlagged tax variable is again highly significant at the 1 per cent level, with $R$ only slightly lowered. The level of shifting for the unlagged tax variable is not greatly affected, but the standard error of the shifting

---

[1] Henceforth the term "highly significant" is used where the statistic passes the two tail $t$ test at the 1 per cent level, significant where it passes at the 5 per cent level, and insignificant where it does not pass even the 5 per cent test.

measure is substantially reduced. The model underlying line 3 is to be preferred. It is adopted as the standard model for the estimation of most other cases.

Various further experiments were made to help appraise the results of line 3. First, the instrument was changed from effective to statutory rates. As shown in line 4, there is little difference in results. Next, an approximation

Table 6–1. Estimates for All Manufacturing

| No. | Description | No. of observations | Intercept $a_0$ | Regression coefficients, [ ] as fraction Variables | | | |
|---|---|---|---|---|---|---|---|
| | | | | $\Delta C_{t-1}$ | $V_{t-1}$ | $J_t$ | $L_t$ |
| (I) | (II) | (III) | (IV) | (V) | (VI) | (VII) | (VIII) |
| 1. | All years | 20 | .2575 | .3844 [2.0930] | −.3443 [−1.9226] | −.9079 [−4.3511] | 1.4516 [7.1688] |
| 2. | All years | 20 | .2577 | .3013 [1.8053] | −.4228 [−2.2586] | −.7721 [−4.4863] | 1.5110 [8.2192] |
| 3. | All years (standard model) | 20 | .2859 | .4038 [2.6690] | −.5272 [−3.0043] | −.8333 [−4.7168] | 1.3394 [12.2165] |
| 4. | All years | 20 | .2815 | .4115 [2.7409] | −.5090 [−2.9259] | −.8341 [−4.7561] | 1.3575 [12.5142] |
| 5. | All years[b] | 20 | n.c. | n.c. | n.c. | n.c. | 1.3373 [n.c.] |
| 6. | All years | 20 | n.c. | .4966 [3.5440] | −.4681 [−3.0253] | −.8967 [−5.4347] | 1.4199 [15.3468] |
| 7. | Prewar | 8 | .3693 | .6458 [1.7166] | −.7776 [−1.8894] | −1.0334 [−1.6006] | 1.3394 [8.3068] |
| 8. | Postwar | 12 | .2698 | .1593 [.5962] | −.1044 [−2.5218] | −1.1223 [−3.1541] | 1.2050 [4.3398] |
| 9. | All years | 20 | .1760 | .1307 [.4123] | −.4988 [−1.2706] | – | 1.0273 [3.6553] |
| 10. | All years (1942 excluded) | 19 | .1210 | −.0124 [−.0042] | −.1963 [−.5862] | – | 1.0395 [4.0804] |
| 11. | All years[g] (1959 excluded) | 17 | .0005 | .3027 [.9714] | −.0351 [−.8855] | −.6423 [−1.5505] | 1.4238 [5.8189] |

  [a] Durbin-Watson statistics. See Appendix E p. 97.

  [b] Based on model B, see no. (4) Table 6–3, p. 50.

  [c] Tables for Durbin-Watson statistics for the case of 6 explanatory variables are not available.

  [d] The series does not pass the Durbin-Watson test for negative serial auto-correlation. The statistics fall in the middle between upper and lower critical levels for the doubtful area.

method was used in place of the instrumental approach.[2] As shown in line 5, the results remain very similar. To check into the high value of $R$ obtained from the instrumental variable approach, use was made of the least-squares

[2] See Klein, *op. cit.*, pp. 120–21. Beginning with the estimate of model B, given in line 3 of Table 6–3, we use the approximation $L_t = Z_t^* Y_{g,t} \sim Y_g . Z_t^* + Z_t^* Y_{g,t} - Z_t^* Y_g.$ and substitute for $L_t$. We then solve for $Y_{g,t}$.

Total Capital Base, Model A

| of standard error | | | Instrument or technique | $R$ adjusted | $d$ stat.[a] | Shifting measure[f], ( ) its standard error | | |
|---|---|---|---|---|---|---|---|---|
| $G_t$ (IX) | $L_{t-1}$ (X) | $B_t$ (XI) | (XII) | (XIII) | (XIV) | For initial period (XV) | For one period lag (XVI) | Combined effect (XVII) |
| −.1174 [−1.2598] | .1966 [1.2599] | − | $Z_t^*$ | .9806 | 2.7859[e] | 1.4516 (.2025) | .1654 .1313 | 1.6174 (.1637) |
| −.1083 [−1.1223] | − | − | $Z_t^*$ | .9800 | 2.9380[d] | 1.5110 (.1838) | − | − |
| − | − | − | $Z_t^*$ | .9765 | 2.7557[d] | 1.3394 (.1096) | − | − |
| − | − | − | $Z_t$ | .9768 | 2.7617[d] | 1.3575 (.1085) | − | − |
| − | − | − | Klein's approx. | .9406 | n.c. | 1.3373 (n.c.) | − | − |
| − | − | − | Naive Least Squares | .9805 | 2.6526[d] | 1.4199 (.0925) | − | − |
| − | − | − | $Z_t^*$ | .9772 | 3.0556[e] | 1.3394 (.1612) | − | − |
| − | − | − | $Z_t^*$ | .9191 | 2.1761[e] | 1.2050 (.2777) | − | − |
| − | − | −.0648 [−.3486] | $Z_t^*$ | .9200 | n.c. | 1.0273 (.2810) | − | − |
| − | − | .5250 [1.5390] | $Z_t^*$ | .9247 | n.c. | 1.0395 (.2547) | − | − |
| −.1998 [−1.5619] | − | − | $Z_t^*$ | .9197 | 3.002 | 1.4238 (.2447) | − | − |

s for Durbin-Watson statistics are not available for cases of less than 15 observation points.
e initial period the significance of the shifting measure is the same as that for the $L_t$ variable coefficient.
, all variables differenced, 1959 excluded.

method treating $L_t$ as predetermined (naïve least squares). As expected, this increased $R$ (line 6) above that of the standard model (line 3).

In lines 7 and 8, the standard model is applied to the pre- and postwar periods separately, to allow for the possibility that reactions differed. It appears that this was not the case. The degree of shifting is slightly lower for both periods taken individually than for the combined period, and the test for homoschedasticity is met.[3]

Table 6–2. Simple Correlation Matrix—All Years
(All Manufacturing, Total Capital Base)

| Vari-ables | $V_{t-1}$ | $J_t$ | $G_t$ | $L_{t-1}$ | $Z_t^*$ | $Z_{t-1}^*$ | $L_t$ | $Y_{g,t}$ |
|---|---|---|---|---|---|---|---|---|
| $\Delta C_{t-1}$ | $-.1918$ | .3837 | $-.4310$ | $-.1041$ | .1723 | .0189 | $-.0994$ | $-.0111$ |
| $V_{t-1}$ | | $-.5926$ | $-.2815$ | $-.6966$ | $-.7265$ | $-.7196$ | $-.6420$ | $-.6538$ |
| $J_t$ | | | .1572 | .5907 | .8033 | .6287 | .3323 | .1853 |
| $G_t$ | | | | .5640 | .5864 | .7224 | .7521 | .5997 |
| $L_{t-1}$ | | | | | .7630 | .7933 | .7634 | .6849 |
| $Z_t^*$ | | | | | | .9091 | .7216 | .5836 |
| $Z_{t-1}^*$ | | | | | | | .9086 | .7877 |
| $L_t$ | | | | | | | | .9496 |

*Interpretation*

We are left with the unexpected result of shifting well in excess of 100 per cent. In interpreting this result, it must be noted first of all that the point estimate reflected in the shifting value of 134 per cent is not the entire information. We know its standard error and may compute confidence limits. Given the standard error of .1096 and 15 degrees of freedom, the 95 per cent confidence limit gives the interval of 111 to 157 per cent for the degree of shifting. The hypothesis of zero shifting is clearly rejected, which is quite in line with how we understand the economy to operate. More surprising and perhaps disturbing is the rejection of the hypothesis of 100 per cent shifting. Even 99 per cent confidence limits give an interval from 102 to 166 per cent, so that the hypothesis of at least 100 per cent shifting is still sustained.

Presently we shall note various reasons why this result should be adjusted downward; but first it may be pointed out that we have no a priori insight which tells us by Palmström logic[4] that such a result *must* be wrong. The

[3] See p. 97.
[4] Reference is to the memorable verse
„Weil, so schliesst er messerscharf,
Nicht sein *kann*, was nicht sein *darf*“,
in Christian Morgenstern, *Die Galgenlieder*, (Berlin: Cassirer, 1937), p. 163.

very considerations which show that the traditional conclusion of zero short-run shifting is not necessarily correct also allow the possibility that shifting might reach or exceed 100 per cent.[5] In particular, two hypotheses may be noted. For one thing, changes in tax rates may be taken as a "signal" among oligopolists for price increases, which may include adjustments for other than tax factors. These other factors may be substantial. Since our model combines them with adjustments to the tax as such, the recorded degree of shifting which measures both adjustments against the tax factor only, could well exceed 100 per cent. For another, firms may be so eager to recoup the tax fully that they overshoot the mark.

Nevertheless, this initial result remains surprising, and one wonders whether the high estimated value of shifting might not be due to shortcomings of the model and the data. As shown in Table 6–2, there is a high degree of positive correlation between $G_t$ and $Z_t^*$, which is an instrument for $L_t$.[6] Moreover, we have noted (see lines 2 and 3 of Table 6–1) that discarding the $G_t$ variable increases the significance of all other coefficients in the model, especially that of $L_t$. This suggests that $G_t$ and $L_t$ are collinear. Hence the tax coefficient is exaggerated by a $G_t$ effect which cannot be separated out.[7] That is to say, our measure is not only one of tax incidence, but is contaminated by influences of budget incidence. If a tax increase was accompanied by increased demand for corporate output, be it because the government redirected demand or because public expenditures were increased and aggregate demand rose—the resulting upward shift in the demand for corporate output may have raised $Y_g$ and cushioned the tax effect on $Y_n$. Thus, the change in $Y_g$ reflects tax shifting in the sense of administered price adjustments, as well as responses to changes in government expenditures. While we cannot separate the two effects, we may note the significance of the $L_t$ and insignificance of the $G_t$ coefficients when both are included (see line 2, Table 6–1). This suggests that the $L_t$ coefficient is much the stronger.[8]

[5] See p. 2.

[6] This situation is not improved if state and local government purchases are included in $G_t$. Use of federal purchases only has the advantage that it is a more clearly exogenous variable and that it shows a positive correlation with $Y_g$, whereas state and local purchases are negatively correlated with $Y_g$.

[7] If our result of high shifting is to be explained by a hidden $G_t$ effect, then the "true" coefficient for $G_t$ should be positive. While the estimated coefficient (lines 1 and 2 of Table 6-1), is negative, this is not too disturbing. Not only is the coefficient insignificant, but the negative value may be due to high correlation with $L_t$, inclusion of both pulling the estimates apart.

[8] We considered the hypothesis that the high correlation of $G_t$ and $Z_t^*$ was due to the fact that in many years both variables remained unchanged. This was tested by differencing the $Z^*$ and $G$ variable, and eliminating the years for which $\Delta Z^* = 0$. The correlation between the two variables on this basis, however, proved as high as before.

In addition to the correlation between $G_t$ and $Z_t^*$, we further find an even higher correlation between $J_t$ and $Z_t^*$. This, however, does not involve collinearity, because the introduction of $J_t$ does not lower the significance of the other coefficient. Nevertheless, the high correlation may pull the estimates of the two coefficients apart, thus increasing the negative value of the $J_t$ coefficient and the positive value of the $L_t$ coefficient. Again our measure may exaggerate the degree of shifting.

An alternative way of allowing for other fiscal factors was attempted by omitting the $G_t$ and $J_t$ variables, but introducing the state of budgetary balance. In lines 9 and 10 the model is re-estimated, substituting a surplus rate $B_t$ for the $G_t$ and $J_t$ variables.[9] On theoretical grounds this is a less satisfactory approach, since the government variables which are treated separately in the standard model are now lumped together. As may be expected, the value of $R$ is lower than before. The coefficient of the $B$ variable, as shown in lines 9 and 10 is insignificant. It is interesting to note, however, that it is positive in line 10 suggesting that the change in the surplus was on the average endogenous, and that it is negative in line 9 suggesting that it was autonomous. Since line 10 differs from line 9 by exclusion of 1942, when the change was highly autonomous, this pattern is plausible. The degree of shifting is now down to about 100 per cent. Since the $B$ variable allows at least partly for the $G$ and $J$ effects, and is notably correlated with $L$, the $L$ coefficient in this model may reflect more purely the tax effect. However, not too much can be made of this, because the model is inferior in terms of multiple $R$ and the significance of the regression coefficients is lowered.

In addition to these difficulties, it may be that our model has omitted a variable which explains $Y_g$ and is highly correlated with $Z_t$. However, this is unlikely, since such a variable would tend to be of the fiscal type, and fiscal variables have been considered.

As another possibility, it might be suggested that for some reasons, not captured specifically in our model, the rate of return had a positive time trend; and that the tax factor, being a variable with rising time trend, is held responsible for it. Leaving aside the question of whether such a time trend in $Y_g$ is plausible, this possible bias would be more or less eliminated by differ-

---

An alternative procedure might have been to include only that sub-sample of years (sufficiently large to give significant results) for which the correlation was least. Unfortunately, this proved not possible because observations sharing dissimilar changes were too infrequent to reduce the correlation coefficient substantially.

[9] The surplus rate $B$ is defined as $G - J - \dfrac{T}{GNP}$, where $G$ is federal purchases divided by $GNP$, $T$ is corporate tax accruals, and $J$ is the ratio of other taxes minus transfers to $GNP$.

encing the model. As shown in Table 6–1, line 11, our result is changed very little by differencing.

Could it be, finally, that the result is affected by inflation? If there is a tendency to increasingly overstate profits relative to capital, $Y_g$ would be overstated and this might be charged to shifting. As shown in the next chapter, the adjustment for inflation—which affects both capital and profit figures—does in fact lower the estimated degree of shifting to about 100 per cent. Moreover, we shall note that this result still tends to overstate the degree of tax shifting because expenditure effects are present. Thus, it appears that pure tax shifting will be below 100 per cent. But even after liberal allowance is made for these factors, the statistical quality of the shifting estimate remains rather impressive, and substantial evidence of a high degree of short-run shifting cannot be denied.[10]

## B. MODEL B

The first three lines of Table 6–3 show results for Model B, corresponding to those for Model A, given in lines 1–3 of Table 6–1. Statutory rates are now used for the tax variable. The estimated degree of shifting is much higher than in Model A, the standard errors of the coefficients are larger, and the significance is substantially lower. The multiple correlation coefficient is lower as well. The picture of Model B worsens further if effective rates are used for the tax variable. As shown in line 4 of Table 6–3, the value of $R$ drops, the shifting measure rises but its significance declines, leading to extremely wide confidence limits. By using the liability-type tax variable, a better fit was obtained in Model A, which suggests its behavioral assumption is more realistic. Model A is to be preferred on all these grounds.

---

[10] It does not follow that shifting must be equally high or speedy whether the tax rises or falls. See p. 58.

Table 6-3. Estimates for All Manufacturing

| No. | Period | No. of ob- serva- tions | Inter- cept $a_0$ | Regression coefficients, [ ] as fractions o | | | |
|---|---|---|---|---|---|---|---|
| | | | | | | | Variable |
| | | | | $\Delta C_{t-1}$ | $V_{t-1}$ | $J_t$ | $X_t$ |
| 1. | All years | 20 | n.c. | .8320 [2.6081] | −1.0027 [−3.2985] | −2.0603 [−3.5989] | .3290 [4.6284] |
| 2. | All years | 20 | n.c. | .8190 [2.6903] | −.9716 [−3.5956] | −2.1704 [−5.7918] | .3298 [4.8068] |
| 3. | All years | 20 | n.c. | .9170 [3.1696] | −1.0451 [−4.0073] | −2.0447 [−5.7687] | .2704 [7.4337] |
| 4. | All years | 20 | n.c. | .6106 [2.0574] | −.6996 [−2.2499] | −2.0046 [−5.2064] | .4072 [6.6602] |

Total Capital Base, Model B

| standard error | | Notation X stands for tax variable | R adjusted | $d^{a}$ stat. | Shifting measure, ( ) its standard error[d] | | |
|---|---|---|---|---|---|---|---|
| $G_t$ | $X_{t-1}$ | | | | For initial period | For one period lag | Combined effect |
| −.1516 [−.6068] | −.0222 [−.2615] | $Z_t$ and $Z_{t-1}$ | .9237 | 2.8082[b] | 2.2922 (.4952) | −.1407 (.5381) | 2.1515 (1.0824) |
| −.1925 [−1.0213] | – | $Z_t$ | .9290 | 2.7919[c] | 2.2978 (.4780) | – | – |
| – | – | $Z_t$ | .9288 | 2.5176[c] | 1.8836 (.2534) | – | – |
| – | – | $Z_t^*$ | .9151 | n.c. | 2.7847 (.4181) | – | – |

[a] Durbin-Watson statistics. See p. 97.
[b] Tables for Durbin-Watson statistics are not available for the case of 6 explanatory variables.
[c] The series does not pass Durbin-Watson test for negative serial auto-correlation. The statistics falls in the middle between upper and lower critical levels for the doubtful area.
[d] For the initial period the significance of the shifting measure is the same as that for $X_t$ variable coefficient.

# CHAPTER 7

# FURTHER RESULTS

WE NOW TURN to a set of further results, including variants of the all-manufacturing case and sub-groups thereof. The model throughout is that of Model A, standard case, line 3, as shown in Table 6–1.

## A. VARIANTS OF THE ALL-MANUFACTURING CASE

The all-manufacturing case is re-estimated allowing for a number of adjustments, including those for accelerated depreciation, inflation, and risk-rate of return. The new results are given in Table 7–1, each case being estimated for the entire period and for the postwar period only.

### Equity Base

Lines 1 and 2 repeat the results of Table 6–1. In line 3 of Table 7–1 the model is placed on an equity base, where the rate of return is defined as the ratio of profits to equity capital. The multiple correlation is slightly less than on the total capital base. The degree of shifting for the entire period is somewhat lower at 123 per cent, with significance somewhat lower as well. At a 95 per cent significance level the confidence limits are from 98 to 148 per cent. The difference between this result and that for the total capital case is not substantial, but it is in agreement with the hypothesis that the small observed rise in debt financing was partially caused by the tax.[1]

### Tax Effects on Internal Funds

There is a substantial body of opinion which holds that the more significant aspect of tax effects is the effect on internally available funds, rather than on

---

[1] Assuming the same profit adjustment to occur in both cases, it also follows from the mathematical relationship that the degree of shifting for the equity case has to be somewhat less.

the rate of return. Our model may be adapted readily to explore this problem. The rate of return variable is redefined to include depreciation, and the degree of shifting is re-estimated on this basis.

The results (all-manufacturing, equity base) are shown in lines 5 and 6 of Table 7–1. The multiple $R$ is somewhat above that of line 3, where the profit rate only is considered. The hypothesis that firms define the target rate of return in terms of total funds is at least as compatible with our model as the earlier hypothesis based on the profit rate. The degree of shifting in line 5 is 146 per cent, as against 123 per cent in line 3. In a situation where part of the tax recoupment is through raising profits while another part is through raising depreciation, the shifting measure in terms of funds should show a higher degree of shifting than that in terms of profits only. Our results are compatible with such a situation.

*Changes in Tax Rate vs. Changes in Statutory Depreciation Rate*

As noted before, Model A is based on the use of observed tax liabilities. Changes in these liabilities depend on both legislative changes in tax rates and in depreciation rates. Our results with regard to shifting, therefore, measure the adjustment to the combined change in tax liability, whatever the cause. They do not measure "tax-rate shifting" alone, but combined "tax-rate" and "depreciation-rate" shifting.

How might the two aspects of the problem be separated? One way would be to use two distinct tax variables, one the statutory tax rate and one the statutory depreciation rate. This, however, would require a model B type approach which proved much inferior. Accepting the fact that we must use observed liabilities as the tax variable, this solution is not open. However, our result for the combined effect may be interpreted to some extent by introducing assumptions regarding firm reactions to depreciation changes.

Consider our usual measure of shifting and suppose first that an increase in depreciation due to a speed up in the statutory depreciation rate is reflected fully in price increase, thus leaving profits unchanged. In this case, our measure of shifting for the profit rate of return (line 3, Table 7–1) will correctly indicate shifting in response to tax-rate change only. If, however, the rise in depreciation due to an increase in the statutory depreciation rate leaves prices unchanged and is reflected fully in a decline in profits, the true degree of shifting in response to tax-rate change exceeds the line 3 measure. The same holds to a lesser degree if the rise in prices due to acceleration falls short of the full amount.

A similar argument holds for the funds approach. If an increase in depreciation due to acceleration is reflected fully in price increases, the funds measure of shifting overstates the degree of shifting attributable to tax-rate changes alone. If the increase in depreciation is absorbed in declining gross profits, the fund measure reflects the effect of tax-rate changes only.

In the case where the rise in depreciation due to acceleration depresses

Table 7–1. Estimates for All Manufacturing,

| No. | Description | No. of observations | Intercept $a_0$ | Regression coefficients, [ ] as fractions | | |
|---|---|---|---|---|---|---|
| | | | | $\Delta C_{t-1}$ | $V_{t-1}$ | $J_t$ |
| I | II | III | IV | V | VI | VII |
| 1. | Total capital base, all years | 20 | .2859 | .4038 [2.6690] | −.5272 [−3.0043] | −.8333 [−4.7168] |
| 2. | No. (1) postwar | 12 | .2698 | .1593 [.5962] | −.1044 [−2.5281] | −1.1223 [−3.1541] |
| 3. | Equity base, all years | 20 | .4234 | .3431 [1.8180] | −.9429 [−4.2971] | −1.1778 [−5.3266] |
| 4. | No. (3) postwar | 12 | .4742 | .06934 [.1923] | −1.1113 [−1.9692] | −1.2206 [−2.5209] |
| 5. | Equity base, dpr. returned to profits all years | 20 | .2707 | .6705 [3.9037] | −.4521 [−2.3027] | −.5409 [−2.6749] |
| 6. | No. (5) postwar | 12 | .2122 | .6161 [2.5936] | .0704 [.1910] | −.6233 [−1.9426] |
| 7. | Equity base, correct for inflation, all years | 20 | .2507 | .0743 [.4062] | −.4848 [−2.1430] | −.6119 [−2.9182] |
| 8. | No. (7) postwar | 12 | .2111 | −.2014 [−.6378] | .1869 [.3259] | −.9737 [−2.2400] |
| 9. | Risk rate, equity base, all years[g] | 20 | .2627 | .6138 [2.7413] | −.4836 [−1.8574] | −.9416 [−3.5892] |
| 10. | No. (9) postwar[g] | 12 | .2129 | .1799 [.4679] | .5668 [.9418] | −1.5894 [−3.0779] |
| 11. | Equity base, all years | 20 | .6334 | .8814 [2.4287] | −1.6811 [−6.1220] | −1.3958 [−3.1677] |

[a] Corresponds to line 3, Table 6–1, with $Z_t^*$ for instrument, except for line 11, where the differential rate $Z_t^{**}$ is used.

[b] Durbin-Watson statistics. See Appendix E p. 97.

[c] The series does not pass the Durbin-Watson test for negative serial auto-correlation. The statistics fall in the middle between upper and lower critical levels for the doubtful area.

[d] Tables for the Durbin-Watson statistics are not available for cases of less than 15 observation points.

[e] The series does not pass the Durbin-Watson test for negative serial auto-correlation. The statistics leave us in doubt but is close to the upper critical level above which there is no doubt that serial auto-correlation is absent.

profits, the true degree of shifting for the profit measure in response to tax-rate changes will fall between our estimated degree of shifting for the profit measure (which, as we have seen, is too low) and the fund measure. This follows because, in a situation of rising depreciation, shifting in profit terms cannot exceed shifting in fund terms. Since we do not know to what extent the rise in depreciation leaves profits unchanged (in which case the profit measure

Model A, Standard[a]

| standard error | | | Instrument | $R$ adjusted | $d$ stat.[b] | Shifting measure,[h] ( ) its standard error | | |
| --- | --- | --- | --- | --- | --- | --- | --- | --- |
| ariables | | | | | | For initial period | For one period lag | Combined effect |
| $L_t$ VIII | $L_t^{**}$ IX | $L_{t-1}^{**}$ X | XI | XII | XIII | XIV | XV | XVI |
| 1.3394 [2.2165] | – | – | $Z_t^*$ | .9765 | 2.7557[c] | 1.3394 (.1096) | – | – |
| 1.2050 [4.3398] | – | – | $Z_t^*$ | .9191 | 2.1761[d] | 1.2050 (.2777) | – | – |
| 1.2331 [0.4348] | – | – | $Z_t^*$ | .9745 | 2.4285[e] | 1.2331 (.1182) | – | – |
| 1.0783 [2.9213] | – | – | $Z_t^*$ | .9048 | 2.2783[d] | 1.0783 (.3691) | – | – |
| 1.4644 [4.3727] | – | – | $Z_t^*$ | .9803 | 2.3368[e] | 1.4644 (.1019) | – | – |
| 1.2688 [6.8367] | – | – | $Z_t^*$ | .9270 | 2.1350[d] | 1.2688 (.1856) | – | – |
| 1.0050 [8.0746] | – | – | $Z_t^*$ | .9580 | 1.9603 | 1.0050 (.1245) | – | – |
| .7848 [2.0120] | – | – | $Z_t^*$ | .8347 | 1.9770[d] | .7848 (.3901) | – | – |
| 1.4154 [0.0955] | – | – | $Z_t^*$ | .9652 | 2.1966[f] | 1.4154 (.1402) | – | – |
| 1.1243 [2.8562] | – | – | $Z_t^*$ | .8730 | 2.0650[d] | 1.1243 (.3936) | – | – |
| – | 1.8008 [5.1820] | .1330 [.2700] | $Z_t^{**}$ for $L_t^{**}$ | .9424 | 2.6144[c] | 1.8008[i] (.3475) | .1072[i] (.3972) | 1.9081[i] (.3250) |

[f] The series does not pass the Durbin-Watson test for negative serial auto-correlation at 5 per cent significance level, but it does at 2½ and 1 per cent level.

[g] Risk rate defined as gross rate of return on equity less the rate on Moody's triple A bonds.

[h] The significance of the shifting measure for the initial period is the same as for the $L_t$ or $L_t^{**}$ variable coefficient.

[i] Shifting of differential rate is defined $S_d = a_L^{**}$ for unlagged variable

$$S_{d-1} = a_{L-1}^{**} \frac{L_{.-1}^{**}}{L_.^{**}} \text{ for lagged variable.}$$

would reflect tax-rate changes only) or depresses profits, the true value for the tax effect on profits will fall between the results of lines 3 and 5 in Table 7–1.

### Adjustment for Inflation

The estimate for the model using the series adjusted for inflation is given in lines 7 and 8 of Table 7–1.[2] The shifting measure is lower for the adjusted case. As shown in line 7, it is now just about 100 per cent. We are tempted to conclude that allowance for the inflation factor may be an alternative way of explaining the appearance of shifting above 100 per cent noted in the preceding chapter.

Interpretation of the inflation adjustment poses a problem somewhat similar to that of changes in the statutory depreciation rate. Suppose that increases in tax rates coincided with inflation-caused increases in the replacement cost of depreciable assets. Now distinguish two cases: (1) where the rise in replacement cost did not affect product prices, and (2) where prices and profits were increased to make up for the short-fall of nominal, behind "true" depreciation. In case (1) our measure of shifting based on the series without inflation adjustment will be correct, while a measure based on data adjusted for inflation would understate true shifting in response to the tax effect alone. In case (2), the unadjusted measure would overstate shifting, especially if the firm reacted sharply to inflation in asset cost and less so to tax increase. The measure of shifting based on the adjusted series would then correctly isolate the tax effect. Whichever case holds, the shifting measure based on the adjusted series should be lower.

As we do not know which behavior applied, the results for the unadjusted series (line 3) and the adjusted series (line 7) may be taken to set the upper and lower limits for the true answer. Allowance for the inflation factor thus results in a substantial drop in the shifting measure. At a 95 per cent confidence level, the limits are between 74 per cent and 127 per cent. While the multiple $R$ for the adjusted series is somewhat smaller and the significance of the tax coefficient is somewhat less, the difference is not substantial, especially if one allows for possible errors introduced through the inflation adjustment.

### Risk Rate of Return

It has been suggested that the firm's target rate of return be defined in terms of the return for risk taking or entrepreneurship, excluding such part

[2] For method of adjustment, see p. 76.

of the gross return as corresponds to the bond rate which, for purposes of our model, is autonomously set. In this case, one may wish to relate the shifting measure to the rate of return in excess of the bond rate. A model based on this approach is shown in lines 9 and 10 of Table 7–1, where the risk rate is defined as the observed gross rate of return on equity minus Moody's triple A bond rate. The R is slightly less than in line 3. The shifting measure is somewhat higher on the risk rate basis. This is as may be expected, since for any given tax liability and increase in the total gross rate of return, the degree of shifting must be higher if related to the risk rate of return only.[3]

### Differential Tax Rate

Various writers, in particular A. C. Harberger, have argued that the relevant rate for the shifting problem is not the corporate rate, but the differential between the rate of tax on profits earned through the corporation and the rate of tax on profits earned through non-corporate investment.[4] This is essentially a longer run view, since the vehicle of shifting is through diversion of capital from the corporate to the non-corporate sector. It is of some interest nevertheless to apply the differential rate approach to our short run model.

In line 11 of Table 7–1, the differential rate, lagged and unlagged, is introduced into the all-manufacturing, equity base model. For this purpose tax liability is redefined as the observed value of L weighted by the ratio of the differential to the corporate tax rate.[5] The differential tax variable is introduced in both lagged and unlagged form, since one may expect the lagged variable to be important in this case. The result does not bear out this expectation. The coefficient for the lagged differential tax variable is insignificant, as was the case in line 1 of Table 6–1, when the total corporate liability was used. The unlagged variable shows a higher degree of shifting than the corporate liability variable in line 1 of Table 6–1, but the multiple R is lower. Errors are higher and significance is reduced.

Considering the fact that the shifting results for the corporate and differential approach are rather similar, which should be accepted as explaining

---

[3] An alternative approach might have been to prorate the tax between the risk and interest component, and to apply the risk component only to the risk rate of return. In this case, equality of the degree of shifting for both components would suggest that the businessman is concerned with the total rate. This inference cannot be drawn from the above model.

[4] See p. 4, note 3.

[5] We have $L_t^{**} = L_t \dfrac{Z_t^{**}}{Z_t^*}$, where $Z_t^{**}$ equals the differential rates given in Col. IX of Table 3–1 and $Z_t^*$ equals the effective corporate rate shown in Col. VI.

the behavior of the economy? Since the adjustment to the differential rate operates through the flow of capital to the unincorporated sector, it may be expected not to occur in the year of rate change and, indeed, extend over more than the subsequent year. Since the lagged variable is insignificant in both approaches, it appears that the adjustment process was essentially in response to the corporate rate. The similarity of the results may be explained by the high correlation (.9 for the unlagged form) between the two tax variables.

### Direction of Tax Rate Change

It is of considerable interest for policy purposes to determine whether the firm's reaction is the same to increases as to decreases in the tax rate. For this purpose, the model was differenced and two tax variables were introduced. One variable is $\triangle L_t$ equal to $\Delta L_t$ for years of rate increase and equal to zero for other years; the other is $\triangle L_t$, equal to $\Delta L_t$ for years of rate decrease and equal to zero for other years. We obtain the following result:

$$\Delta Y_{gt} = .0149 + .8467\Delta^2 C_{t-1} - .6381\Delta V_{t-1} - .0205\Delta J_t + 1.6920\triangle L_t +$$
$$\qquad\qquad [1.8992] \qquad [-1.4945] \qquad [-.0404] \qquad [3.2811]$$
$$\qquad\qquad\qquad\qquad\qquad\qquad\qquad\qquad + .0704\triangle L_t + U_t \qquad R = .8584$$
$$\qquad\qquad\qquad\qquad\qquad\qquad\qquad\qquad\quad [.0530]$$

Multiple correlation is lower than for the combined $L$ variable, as is the significance of the tax variable coefficients. The $\triangle L$ coefficient remains highly significant, while the $\triangle L$ becomes totally insignificant. The estimated degree of shifting for the positive change is 170 per cent, but for the negative change is only 7 per cent. This supports the hypothesis that short-run shifting in response to a tax increase is much stronger than is "un-shifting" in response to a tax decrease. In fact, our result suggests zero un-shifting.

To be more exact, our model shows the result of no or slight un-shifting for the immediate period of rate change only. It is possible that un-shifting occurs with a time lag, even though shifting (in the case of rate increase) results in the same period.[6]

### B.  SUBGROUPS

So far the discussion has been in terms of all-manufacturing as a whole. We now turn to the results for certain subgroups thereof, the results being given in Table 7–2. Throughout, we use the formulation of the standard model, given in line 3 of Table 6–1.

---

[6] Again the sample does not permit us to test whether this asymmetry reflects differences in the correlation of the expenditure and tax variables for cases of tax increase and decrease.

## Size Groups

Total manufacturing was divided into companies with assets above and below $50 million. The results are given in lines 1–4 of Table 7–2. The equity base is used. Taking the period as a whole, the multiple correlation for the two size groups is about the same as for the combined group, as shown in line 3, Table 7–1. The degree of shifting is 121 per cent for the large and 129 per cent for the small asset group, as against 123 per cent for the combined group. The somewhat higher degree of shifting for the smaller group is contrary to expectation, but the difference is slight. Considering the postwar period only, the value of *R* drops sharply for the smaller group. Estimated shifting drops to 49 per cent and is insignificant. For the larger group, the postwar picture does not differ greatly from that for the entire period.

## Industry Groups

Without making a comprehensive attempt at industry analysis, our model was applied also to a few industry groups. While an intensive analysis of subgroups and individual firms might call for different models in each case, or different variables than in the type of model here used, no such attempt was made. The general model was applied for subgroups and, as shown in Table 7–2, the explanatory value remained quite high. The total capital base was used and the results are recorded in lines 5 to 14 of Table 7–2. We begin with the period as a whole. With the exception of pulp and paper, the values of *R* are high, and the estimated degree of shifting ranges from 125 per cent for stone, clay, and glass to 158 per cent for pulp and paper. There is also a substantial variation in the significance of the shifting measure. The lack of uniformity in the shifting pattern is not surprising, considering the wide variety of industrial structures and market conditions. However, our industry analysis is much too limited to permit a systematic discussion of this aspect.

Considering the postwar period only, the values of *R* are less and the pattern is more varied. The estimated degrees of shifting are generally lower, with estimated shifting especially low and insignificant for pulp and paper and for food and kindred products.

In addition to these complete industry groups, consideration was given also to a sample of 26 steel companies and a sample of 12 textile companies. The results are shown in lines 15 to 18 of Table 7–2. For the period as a whole, the estimated degree of shifting is 127 and 123 per cent for the two cases respectively, but significance is less in the textile case which also has a lower

Table 7–2. Estimates for Industries, Samples of Companies,

| No. | Description | No. of ob-serva-tions | Regression | |
|---|---|---|---|---|
| | | | Inter-cept $a_0$ | $\Delta C_{t-1}$ |
| I | II | III | IV | V |
| 1. | Equity base, assets $>50$ M, all years | 19[e] | .4268 | .4535 [2.3752] |
| 2. | No. (1) postwar | 11[e] | .3474 | .1875 [.5149] |
| 3. | Equity base, assets $<50$ M, all years | 19[e] | .3541 | .3446 [1.5872] |
| 4. | No. (3) postwar | 11[e] | .5448 | −.1387 [−.1683] |
| 5. | Leather, hide, and products, total capital base, all years | 20 | .2859 | .4761 [2.6891] |
| 6. | No. (5) postwar | 12 | .2902 | .2026 [.6018] |
| 7. | Rubber and products, total capital base, all years | 20 | .1946 | .6067 [4.5316] |
| 8. | No. (7) postwar | 12 | .1517 | .4571 [2.0238] |
| 9. | Pulp and paper, total capital base, all years | 20 | .0919 | .4118 [1.9167] |
| 10. | No. (9) postwar | 12 | .1191 | .5813 [1.2252] |
| 11. | Food and kindred products, total capital base, all years | 20 | .1510 | .2927 [4.7217] |
| 12. | No. (11) postwar | 12 | .1863 | .3871 [2.1576] |
| 13. | Stone, clay and glass, total capital base, all years | 20 | .3889 | .7168 [4.5145] |
| 14. | No. (13) postwar | 12 | .3695 | .3495 [1.5110] |
| 15. | 26 steel companies, equity base, all years | 19 | .4594 | .7223 [2.1300] |
| 16. | No. (15) postwar | 12 | .3977 | .4516 [.8653] |
| 17. | 12 textile companies, equity base, all years | 19 | .5300 | .7377 [1.3818] |
| 18. | No. (17) postwar | 12 | .2845 | −.0570 [−.0921] |
| 19. | 15 largest, price leaders, equity base, all years | 19 | .3802 | .6601 [3.6791] |
| 20. | No. (19) postwar | 12 | .3619 | .2436 [.9629] |
| 21. | 15 largest, price followers, equity base, all years | 18[j] | .4914 | .4334 [1.6946] |
| 22. | No. (21) postwar | 12 | .3959 | .1332 [.3966] |
| 23. | General Motors, equity base, all years | 19 | .9592 | 1.4972 [2.4463] |
| 24. | No. (25) postwar | 12 | .8252 | .3862 [.4465] |
| 25. | U.S. Steel, equity base, all years | 19 | .1133 | .5963 [2.1976] |
| 26. | No. (26) postwar | 12 | .1794 | 1.3140 [2.8994] |

*See page 62 for footnotes.*

d Individual Companies, Model A, Standard[a]

| efficients [ ] as fractions of standard error | | | R adjusted | d stat.[b] | Shifting measure ( ) its standard error[c] |
|---|---|---|---|---|---|
| Variables | | | | | |
| $V_{t-1}$ VI | $J_t$ VII | $L_t$ VIII | IX | X | XI |
| −1.0055 [−3.7852] | −1.0636 [−4.4941] | 1.2115 [8.7183] | .9764 | 2.1213 | 1.2115 (.1390) |
| −.1618 [−.1269] | −1.4409 [−3.0985] | 1.1688 [4.4517] | .9152 | 1.7027[d] | 1.1688 (.2626) |
| −.6632 [−2.5285] | −1.1285 [−4.4711] | 1.2894 [10.4945] | .9740 | 2.6253[f] | 1.2894 (.1229) |
| −1.3134 [−.4645] | −1.1336 [−1.2409] | .4186 [.3000] | .4604 | 2.0613[d] | .4186 (1.3952) |
| −.6675 [−2.7559] | −.6490 [−3.0002] | 1.3374 [8.5002] | .9768 | 2.9246[f] | 1.3374 (.1573) |
| −.1893 [−.3674] | −1.1499 [−2.6211] | 1.2685 [6.0887] | .9420 | 2.1763[d] | 1.2685 (.2083) |
| −.2473 [−1.6145] | −.6562 [−3.6442] | 1.5512 [15.0258] | .9872 | 2.9035[f] | 1.5512 (.1032) |
| .0972 [.2833] | −.7308 [−2.3563] | 1.4972 [13.0432] | .9760 | 2.8569[d] | 1.4972 (.1148) |
| .0604 [.2280] | −.4283 [−1.6564] | 1.5770 [6.0685] | .9144 | 1.6264[g] | 1.5770 (.2599) |
| .7780 [1.0452] | −.9217 [−1.7623] | .2807 [.1906] | .6360 | 2.5672[d] | .2807 (1.4722) |
| −.0655 [−.8538] | −.6265 [−7.8169] | 1.5412 [18.0637] | .9872 | 2.0564 | 1.5412 (.0853) |
| −.0675 [−.3314] | −.3983 [−1.6480] | .4044 [.6227] | .8279 | 2.7773[d] | .4044 (.6495) |
| −.8923 [−4.0608] | −.9502 [−4.8461] | 1.2507 [10.1755] | .9825 | 2.2392 | 1.2507 (.1229) |
| −.2953 [−.7856] | −1.4914 [−4.7342] | 1.2827 [8.3467] | .9681 | 2.2745[d] | 1.2827 (.1537) |
| −1.1167 [−2.6986] | −1.0820 [−2.7306] | 1.2664 [9.6720] | .9632 | 1.8934 | 1.2264 (.1309) |
| −.5079 [−.6092] | −1.3160 [−1.8547] | 1.2219 [6.6743] | .9385 | 2.0556[d] | 1.2219 (.1831) |
| −.9666 [−1.5129] | −1.8322 [−2.6544] | 1.2264 [4.7203] | .9262 | 2.8535 | 1.2264 (.2598) |
| .5770 [.6508] | −2.2091 [−1.3717] | 1.7512 [2.5806] | .9592 | 1.3030[d] | 1.7512 (.6786) |
| −.9997 [−4.0164] | −.5136 [−2.2995] | 1.1106 [10.0343] | .9809 | 2.1430 | 1.1106 (.1107) |
| −.3765 [−.9551] | −1.0664 [−3.1221] | 1.1089 [7.9976] | .9527 | 1.9559[d] | 1.1089 (.1386) |
| −1.2654 [−3.4223] | −.8220 [−2.6632] | .8946 [5.3990] | .9509 | 1.1469[h] | .8946 (.1657) |
| −.5882 [−1.0864] | −1.1671 [−2.5410] | 1.1758 [6.2793] | .9568 | 2.3428[d] | 1.1758 (.1873) |
| −2.2758 [−2.7107] | −2.2112 [−3.0436] | 1.0850 [6.5133] | .9600 | 1.7089[i] | 1.0855 (.1666) |
| −.3929 [−.3017] | −3.6038 [−3.0337] | 1.2181 [7.9014] | .9591 | 1.7661[d] | 1.2181 (.1542) |
| −.3057 [−.6130] | −.1395 [−.3524] | 1.5689 [5.0212] | .9663 | 1.8411[g] | 1.5689 (.3125) |
| −1.6286 [−2.0391] | 1.2826 [1.8391] | .9661 [3.8729] | .9321 | 2.6443[d] | .9661 (.2445) |

multiple $R$.[7] Taking the postwar period only, the estimated degree of shifting for textiles rises to 175 per cent, but the error is more than double as well. The estimate remains significant.

### Price Leaders and Followers

In lines 19 to 22 of Table 7–2 we record the results for two samples of the largest firms, one containing companies which might be considered price leaders, and another containing firms which are more of the price-follower type.[8] The estimate for the leader group shows high multiple correlation and estimated shifting for the period as a whole of 111 per cent. Price followers show a smaller $R$ and an estimated shifting of 89 per cent. There is little difference in the degree of shifting for the postwar period only.

It is surprising that the firms in these samples, all of which are quite large, should show a lesser degree of shifting than obtained previously for all-manufacturing. This, however, is in line with the analysis for the two manufacturing size groups, which also failed to support the hypothesis that large firms shift more.

### Individual Companies

Finally, the analysis was applied to two companies, General Motors and U.S. Steel. The results are given in lines 23 to 26 of Table 7–2. Taking the total period, both companies show a high multiple $R$. The estimated shifting is 109 per cent for General Motors and 157 per cent for U.S. Steel. In the postwar period, the multiple $R$ for U.S. Steel declines somewhat and shifting falls to 97 per cent. In the General Motors case, the shifting rises to 122 per cent.

[7] To permit comparison, an attempt was made to analyze the textiles and apparel group as presented in *Statistics of Income*, but the standard model failed to predict the rate of return, as may be the case with such a heterogeneous group. The industry data for steel was not available on a readily usable basis.

[8] See p. 60.

---

Footnotes to Table 7–2.

[a] Corresponds to line 3, Table 6–1, with $Z_t^*$ for instrument.

[b] Durbin-Watson statistics. See Appendix E. p. 97.

[c] The significance of the shifting measure is the same as for the $L_t$ variable coefficient.

[d] Tables for the Durbin-Watson statistics are not available for cases with less than 15 observation points.

[e] Data for 1959 year were not available.

[f] The series does not pass the Durbin-Watson test for negative serial auto-correlation. The statistics fall in the middle between upper and lower critical levels for the doubtful area.

[g] The series does not pass the Durbin-Watson test for positive serial auto-correlation but only at the 5 per cent level. The statistic leaves us in doubt that serial auto-correlation is absent.

[h] The series does not pass the Durbin-Watson test for positive serial auto-correlation. The statistics falls in the middle between upper and lower critical levels for the doubtful area.

[i] The series does not pass the Durbin-Watson test for positive serial auto-correlation at the 5 and 2½ per cent level but passes at the 1 per cent level.

[j] As the average rate for 1938 was negative, 1938 year has been omitted.

# CHAPTER 8

# CONCLUSIONS

IN THE CONCLUDING CHAPTER the early results will be compared with those of the model, and some policy implications of our results will be noted.

*Differences in Approach*

In Table 8–1 we compare the results of Chapters 6 and 7 with those of Chapter 2. There are two sharp differences between the two approaches:

1. The results of Chapter 2 are based on the crude assumption that the observed changes in the rate of return are due to tax factors only, i.e., they involve an extreme *caeteris-paribus* assumption. The results of Chapters 6 and 7 are estimated on the basis of a model which attempts to isolate the effects of tax rate changes.

2. The observations of Chapter 2 cover several decades, a time span sufficiently long for "long-run" adjustments, including changes in capital stock to occur. The econometric estimates are designed to record the effects of tax-rate changes in the very years of change. While some lagged effects may creep in, the results very largely reflect "short-run" types of adjustment in prices, costs, and output, rather than "long-run" adjustments through changes in capital stock.

*Comparison of Rate of Return Results.*

Given the entirely different approaches it is striking to find that the respective results for all manufacturing, and even for some of the subgroups, are so much alike. In trying to explain this similarity, let us read the results of the model in terms of 100 per cent shifting and assume that we have truly isolated the tax effects.[1]

---

[1] For an evaluation of our estimated results, see pp. 46–51.

Table 8–1.  Estimated Degrees of Shifting

| | General observations, rate-of-return indicator[a] | | Model A[b] | |
|---|---|---|---|---|
| | 1955–57 with 1927–29 | 1955–57 with 1936–39 | All years | Postwar |
| All Manufacturing | | | | |
| Equity | 124 | 136 | 123 | 108 |
| Total Capital | 134 | 134 | 134 | 121 |
| Equity, with inflation correction | n.c. | 99 | 101 | 78 |
| Equity, assets above $50 million | 124 | 121 | 121 | 117 |
| Equity, assets below $50 million | 141 | 129 | 129 | 42 |
| Other Groups | | | | |
| 15 largest firms, price leaders | 147 | 111 | 111 | 111 |
| 15 largest firms, price followers | 140 | 89 | 89 | 118 |
| 26 Steel companies | n.c. | 157 | 123 | 122 |
| 12 Textile companies | n.c. | 21 | 123 | 175 |

  a See Table 2–6, Chapter 2. Shifting based on assumptions that observed changes in rates of return were due to tax factors only.
  b See Tables 7–1 and 7–2. Model A, standard case.

It follows that depressing short-run effects on the rate of return are immediately recouped.  Hence, there will be no long-run depressing effects on the capital stock, whatever the elasticity of its supply.[2]  The increase in the gross rate of return accomplished in the short run stays in the picture and is reflected in the long-run results for the rate of return indicator of Chapter 2. The missing link in the argument is the assumption that the longer-run type of non-tax effects on the gross rate of return washed out and did not affect the averages for the periods compared in Chapter 2.  This assumption cannot be proven here, but it is not unreasonable in the light of recent discussions on economic growth.  Indeed, this line of reasoning is more plausible than other explanations that reject the hypothesis of high short-run shifting and would explain the long-run result by either (a) strong non-tax factors pushing up the rate of return, (b) highly depressing tax effects on the level of capital formation, or (c) a highly elastic response of the marginal productivity of capital to changes in capital stock.

  [2] The recoupment of the corporate tax, by raising prices of corporate products relative to other prices, may lead to a shift in consumer demand toward the non-corporate sector. This may call forth corresponding capital flows. As a result the gross rate of return to capital (in all sectors) may fall, especially if the unincorporated sector is less capital-intensive. (Such capital flows will be much less, however, than those which would be needed if there was no initial price adjustment in the corporate sector, this being the case considered by Harberger, *op. cit.* note 3, p. 4).  This would not show up in our short-run model, but might result in a somewhat lesser degree of shifting in the long-run model.

## Rate of Return vs. Share Results

We return to reconciling the rate of return results of Chapter 2 (now interpreted as being due to short-run type of adjustments) which show 100 per cent shifting with the share results of that chapter which show 40 per cent shifting. Given 100 per cent short-run shifting, the tax did not affect the capital stock. Why then did the gross share not rise at the same rate as did the gross rate of return? As noted in Chapter 2, this might be explained by the nature of the production function which (with a growing capital stock) could depress the capital share more strongly than the gross rate of return.[3] Another possibility was that investors raised their net rate of return target, which retarded capital growth. It may be added now that the government expenditure effect which is not neutralized in our measure of rate-of-return shifting tends to be self-neutralizing in the share measure, as wages as well as profits are affected by government expenditures. Finally, wages may respond to the price rise caused by short-run shifting, so that the share indicator may again show less shifting than the rate of return indicator. All this, to be sure, is speculation only. What is needed is a further study attacking the share indicator directly.[4]

## Policy Implications

Finally, we briefly indicate some of the rather unorthodox policy conclusions which follow from the hypothesis that an increase in the tax is shifted fully through short-run adjustments to prevent a decline in the net rate of return, and that these adjustments are maintained subsequently.

[3] See p. 20. Also see K. J. Arrow, H. B. Chenery, B. S. Minhas, and R. M. Solow, "Capital-Labor Substitution and Economic Efficiency," *The Review of Economics and Statistics*, XLIII, August, 1961, p. 246.

[4] An attempt was made to re-estimate the Model A case given in line 3 of Table 6–1, using as dependent variable the gross profit share for the total corporate sector, as defined in line 9 of Table 2–4. (Use is made of annual data, similar to those of Table 6–1, but ending in 1957). We obtain

$$F_{g,t} = .4050 + .2325 \, \Delta C_{t-1} - .7583 \, V_{t-1} - .7687 \, J_{t-1} + .8970 \, L_t$$
$$[1.0014] \qquad [-2.5440] \quad [-2.7224] \quad [5.3359]$$

$R$ adjusted for degrees of freedom is .9527 and the corresponding measure of shifting is

$$S = \frac{F_{g.} - F'}{F_{g.}} = .7914.$$

In comparing this estimate of 79 per cent share shifting with our higher estimate of rate-of-return shifting, note that the former applies to all corporations whereas the latter applies to all manufacturing only. In comparing the result of .79 with the Chapter 2 result of 40 per cent, note that the estimate of .79 per cent relates to short-run effects, whereas the latter may include long-run results.

1. An increase in the corporate tax rate does not depress growth via the rate-of-return or available-funds type of incentive responses.

2. Equality in the treatment of dividend with other types of income, even if one accepts the partnership view of the corporation, does not call for any kind of dividend relief. No double taxation occurs.

3. The need for integrating retained earnings into the individual income tax base remains, but has to be implemented at the individual level, be it through the partnership or full taxation of capital gains method.

4. The distributional implications of the corporation tax are more or less similar to those of a general sales tax on both corporate capital and consumer goods. The corporation tax, therefore, does not render the tax structure more progressive.

5. The analogy is to a sales tax not at a uniform *ad valorem* rate, but at a rate related to the profit margin of corporations. Thus relative prices are changed by the tax.

6. Points 1–5 have been stated in terms of the consequences of a tax increase. Given the very tentative hypothesis, suggested by our results, that there is no speedy "un-shifting" in the case of rate decrease, it further appears that a reduction in the tax increases profitability, initially at least, and hence may encourage capital formation via the incentive arguments. The distributive gain is to profits rather than wage earners or consumers. These consequences of rate reduction may be significant, even if failure to un-shift is only temporary.

Such is the stark outline of the major policy conclusions which follow if the hypothesis of 100 per cent short-run shifting is accepted. While this hypothesis is supported by our result for the all-manufacturing case, corrected for inflation, several reasons—especially failure to separate government expenditure effects—suggest that this result overstates the degree of short-run shifting. To this extent these policy conclusions need to be softened. But allowing for all the difficulties and qualifications involved, the fact remains that the statistical quality of the shifting estimate is rather impressive. There is substantial evidence for a high degree of short-run shifting, and the policy implications thereof should be faced.

# APPENDICES

# A

# SOURCES OF DATA

A Description of the various data is given in this Appendix, and the actual data for the all-manufacturing case are shown in Tables A–1 and A–2. The analysis uses both industry data and data for individual firms.

*Industry Data*

The industry data is taken from the U.S. Treasury Department, *Statistics of Income, Corporation Returns*, beginning with 1935 and ending with 1959.[1] Inclusion of the first half of the thirties was undesirable since the depression years involved abnormal relations, not readily explainable by a linear analysis. Inclusion of the twenties would have been desirable, but the necessary details are not available for the predepression years.

The data used include the required balance sheet and income statement items for various industry groups. All companies reporting are included, whether with or without income. The inclusion of loss companies introduces some non-homogeneity into our aggregates, but this disturbance is small since a great majority of companies enjoyed profits for most of the years covered. Exclusion of loss companies would introduce a new type of non-homogeneity, as the group of companies included would then change over time. Moreover, the loss problem would not be wholly eliminated because of the carry-over of losses to be charged against future income.

---

[1] Only preliminary data for 1959 were available, hence the data for size groups (with assets over 50 Million, or under 50 Million) end with 1958.

The coverage is consistent over time for such broad groupings as all manufacturing. The more specific groupings (2 digit industries) are often less satisfactory in this respect, as classifications change over time, and broader groups are split into more narrowly defined industries. The subgroups here chosen are some of those for which coverage was held unchanged over our time period. A reworking of the *Statistics of Income* data, to allow for more industry groups with consistent coverage over time, remains to be undertaken.

### Firm Data

In obtaining data for individual firms, the choice was between data published by *SEC* and by *Moody's*. For reasons of easier accessibility, data from *Moody's* were used. Essentially, they are the same as those submitted to the *SEC*. The first full set of *SEC* data is available for 1935, the same being the case for comparable data from *Moody's*. Our firm data, accordingly, begin with 1936 and extend to 1959.

The data for each individual firm had to be appraised and adjusted, when necessary, so as to be comparable over time and between firms. For example, corporate income tax credits, recorded in *Moody's* whenever received, had to be redistributed to years over which they accrued. Changes from consolidated reporting to non-consolidated reporting and vice versa called for adjustment. Interest charges, lumped together in some years with "other costs," had to be separated out and estimated. Depreciation charges, if in excess of those allowed for by tax rules, had to be lowered and profits increased accordingly.

Where these and similar adjustments were not possible, or the firm reports were not comparable over time, the firm was removed from the population of firms under study. This was usually the case if two firms of about equal size merged, thus losing their identity. Also persistent loss companies (a characteristic of many firms in the textile industry) were so removed.

The firm data was used to study the behavior of individual firms and to consider various industry samples. In both respects, only first steps are taken in this study.

### Time Coverage

So far the availability of comparable data set the span of our analysis from 1935 or 1936 to the latest published data in *Statistics of Income* and, for some series, in *Moody's*. It was decided further to exclude the years from 1943 to 1946, a period during which abnormal conditions prevailed due to price control and other reasons. The remaining pre- and postwar years were then treated as a whole. To be sure, it may be doubted whether businessmen's behavior was the same for the pre- and postwar periods.

Tax rates were much lower prewar than postwar, and firms' reactions to tax changes might have changed with the general level of rates. Since there was some doubt regarding the general homogeneity of pre- and postwar data, the analysis was applied also to the postwar period only. As we noted before,[2] the degree of shifting did not differ much from that applicable to the entire period. Use of the postwar period only, however, reduced the degrees of freedom, usually causing the errors of our estimates to rise.

Further loss of observations resulted from the need to lag the capital data to represent the capital at the beginning of the year, and the need to experiment with lagging the tax variable at least one period; thus the time coverage shrunk to:

|  | *Prewar Period* | *Postwar Period* |
|---|---|---|
| (a) industry data | 1936–42 | 1948–59[3] |
| (b) firm data | 1937–42 | 1948–59 |

*Cases*

The cases estimated may be grouped into:

a. Equity Base, where the dependent variable is the ratio of profits to the value of equity capital.
b. Total Capital Base, where the dependent variable is the ratio of profits plus interest paid to equity capital plus interest bearing debt.

The equity-base cases involve four variants:

1. data left unadjusted,
2. data adjusted for inflation,
3. data adjusted to internal funds approach by adding depreciation to profits,
4. data adjusted to risk-rate of return approach by deducting bond rate from the rate of return.

Specifically the following cases were considered:

[2] See tables 7–1, 7–2, pp. 59 and 60.
[3] All-Manufacturing companies with assets over $50 million, and All-Manufacturing companies with assets under $50 million cover the period for 1948–58 only.

*Based on Industry Data*

1. All-Manufacturing, total capital base, all years
2. No. (1), prewar[4]
3. No. (1), postwar
4. All-Manufacturing, equity base, all years
5. No. (4), postwar
6. All-Manufacturing, equity base adjusted for bond rate, all years
7. No. (6), postwar
8. All-Manufacturing, equity base, depreciation returned to profits all years
9. No. (8), postwar
10. All-Manufacturing, equity base corrected for inflation, all years
11. No. (10), postwar
12. All-Manufacturing, equity base with assets over 50 million,[5] all years
13. No. (12)[5], postwar
14. All-Manufacturing, equity base, with assets under 50 million,[5] all years
15. No. (14)[5], postwar
16. Pulp and Paper, total capital base, all years
17. No. (16), postwar
18. Rubber and Products, total capital base, all years
19. No. (18), postwar
20. Leather, Hide and Products, total capital base, all years
21. No. (20), postwar
22. Food and Kindred Products, total capital base, all years
23. No. (22), postwar
24. Stone, Clay, and Glass total capital base, all years
25. No. (24), postwar

*Based on A Sample of Companies*

1. 26 Steel Companies, equity base, all years
2. No. (1), postwar
3. 12 Textile Companies, equity base, all years
4. No. (3), postwar
5. 15 Largest, Price Leaders, equity base, all years
6. No. (5), postwar
7. 15 Largest, Price Followers, equity base, all years
8. No. (7), postwar

[4] Used only to test homoschedasticity of case 1.
[5] 1959 not covered.

The sample of Steel Companies consists of the following 26 companies chosen by random procedure out of a larger population of steel companies in operation over our period:

| | |
|---|---|
| 1. Acme Steel | 14. Laclede Steel |
| 2. American Chain & Cable | 15. National Steel |
| 3. Armco Steel | 16. Pittsburgh Forgings |
| 4. Atlas Tack | 17. Pittsburgh Steel |
| 5. Bethlehem Steel | 18. Poor and Company |
| 6. Bliss & Laughlin | 19. Republic Steel |
| 7. Borg & Warner | 20. Simonds Saw and Steel |
| 8. Continental Steel | 21. Standard Tube Company |
| 9. Copperweld Steel | 22. U.S. Steel |
| 10. Granite City Steel | 23. Vanadium Corp. of America |
| 11. Interlake Iron | 24. Wheeling Steel |
| 12. Inland Steel | 25. Woodward Iron |
| 13. Jones & Laughlin | 26. Youngstown Steel and Tube |

The sample of textile companies includes the following 12 firms, the only companies left after excluding persistent loss companies or companies lacking uniform coverage over time.

| | |
|---|---|
| 1. Adams Mills | 7. Celanese Corporation of America |
| 2. American Hairs & Felt | 8. Graniteville |
| 3. American Manufacturing | 9. Industrial Rayon |
| 4. Belding-Hemingway | 10. Kendall Company |
| 5. Berkshire Hathaway | 11. Mt. Vernon Mills |
| 6. Cannon Mills | 12. National Automotive Fibers |

To choose a sample of the 30 largest companies, we begin with the 100 largest industrial corporations ranked by asset value in the *Fortune Directory* of 1956. From these, 26 were chosen because they were also among the 100 largest firms in 1935 and in 1948, as given by A. D. H. Kaplan, *Big Enterprise in a Competitive Society*, pp. 153–54. Two more companies, among the 100 largest in 1956, were included though they did not rank among the 100 largest in 1935. However, their asset values for both 1935 and 1948 were within 60 per cent of the 100th company. Two additional companies were selected because their asset values for both 1935 and 1948 were within 60 per cent of the 100th company. Thus the criterion of consistently large was preserved.

Further, in arriving at the 30 firm sample we excluded (a) all petroleum, mining, and distilling companies, because of special tax treatment, and (b) a number of other companies[6] because of incompatibility of data.

---

[6] General Electric, Aluminum Company of America, International Harvester Co., Proctor and Gamble, National Dairy Products, U.S. Rubber, and B. F. Goodrich.

Finally the 30 companies were evaluated according to their pricing policy, dividing them into the 15 largest judged to be mostly in the nature of price leaders, and the remaining 15 largest, judged to be more in the nature of price followers.[7]

The sample of the 15 largest, price leader-type firms consists of:

1. American Can
2. American Tobacco
3. Bethlehem Steel
4. Borden
5. Continental
6. Dupont
7. General Motors
8. Goodyear Tire & Rubber
9. International Paper
10. Pittsburgh Plate Glass
11. Radio Corporation of America
12. Swift & Co.
13. Union Carbide Company
14. U.S. Steel
15. Westinghouse Electric

The sample of the 15 largest, price follower-type firms consists of:

1. Allied Chemical and Die
2. Armco Steel
3. Armour and Company
4. Chrysler Corp.
5. Deere & Co.
6. Firestone Tire and Rubber
7. Inland Steel
8. Jones and Laughlin Steel
9. Monsanto Chemical
10. National Lead
11. National Steel
12. Owen Illinois Glass
13. Republic Steel
14. St. Regis Paper
15. Youngstown Sheet and Tube

*Individual Company Data:*

1. General Motors, equity base, all years
2. No. (1), postwar
3. U.S. Steel, equity base, all years
4. No. (3), postwar

*Other Data*

From the basic data referred to, and given in Table A–1 for the all-manufacturing case, the variables $Y_{g,t}$, $L_t$, $L_{t-1}$, and $Z_t^*$ were computed for each series, as shown in Table A–2. The remaining variables $\Delta C_{t-1}$, $V_{t-1}$, $J_t$, $G_t$, $B_t$

[7] In the process of selection, Professor R. F. Lanzillotti of Michigan State University was consulted.

Table A–1.  All Manufacturing, Basic Data, in Billions of Current Dollars.[a]

| Years (1) | Gross profits (2) | Tax liability (3) | Interest paid (4) | Equity[b] (5) | Interest bearing debt (6) |
|---|---|---|---|---|---|
| 1935 | 1.832 | .355 | .338 | 38.152 | 6.036[d] |
| 1936 | 3.614 | .587 | .325 | 37.610 | 6.580[d] |
| 1937 | 3.669 | .641 | .367 | 38.467 | 6.384[d] |
| 1938 | 1.601 | .372 | .321 | 41.240 | 7.497 |
| 1939 | 3.559 | .629 | .338 | 41.260 | 7.533 |
| 1940 | 5.302 | 1.544 | .353 | 42.437 | 7.421 |
| 1941 | 10.300 | 4.881 | .343 | 44.164 | 7.434 |
| 1942 | 13.544 | 8.158 | .415 | 48.397 | 8.470 |
| 1948 | 17.981 | 6.760 | .575 | 76.675 | 13.740 |
| 1949 | 14.154 | 5.446 | .637 | 84.083 | 15.608 |
| 1950 | 23.604 | 10.575 | .622 | 88.885 | 15.378 |
| 1951 | 24.693 | 14.060 | .789 | 97.041 | 16.853 |
| 1952 | 20.223 | 11.348 | .991 | 104.725 | 21.935 |
| 1953 | 21.283 | 12.054 | 1.080 | 109.496 | 25.945 |
| 1954 | 18.184 | 9.385 | 1.082 | 113.813 | 26.866 |
| 1955 | 25.802 | 12.891 | 1.152 | 119.254 | 27.767 |
| 1956 | 24.488 | 12.209 | 1.367 | 130.993 | 29.215 |
| 1957 | 22.653 | 11.431 | 1.630 | 138.988 | 34.805 |
| 1958 | 18.400 | 9.377 | 1.751 | 146.275 | 37.675 |
| 1959[c] | 24.982 | 12.433 | 1.991 | 154.850 | 39.595 |

[a] Based on *Statistics of Income, Corporations Returns*, companies with and without income.
[b] Book values of stock and of undistributed surplus as recorded for the end of the preceding period.
[c] Based on preliminary data.
[d] Estimated.

are common to all cases.  $C_t$ is defined as the ratio of total consumption expenditures to gross national product in 1959 prices, see *Economic Report of the President*, January 1960, Table D–2, p. 156.  $V_t$ is defined as the ratio of sales to inventories in manufacturing.  For the years beginning 1939, the values are obtained from *Economic Report of the President*, Janaury 1960, Table D–34, p. 196.  For the years preceding 1939, sales and inventories series were obtained from *Statistics of Income* and scaled so as to join with the other series in 1939.  $J_t$ is defined as the ratio of federal, state, and local tax receipts, excluding corporate tax accruals, minus transfers and grant in aid to state and local governments to GNP.  The series was obtained from *U.S. Income and Output*, 1958, Table III; n. 164–65, supplemented by *Survey of Current Business*, February, 1961, Table 7, p. 13, for years 1958 and 1959. $G_t$ is defined as the ratio of Federal purchases to GNP, given in *Economic Report of the President*, January 1960, Table TD–2, pp. 156–57.  $B_t$ is the ratio of the surplus or deficit for all levels of government to GNP, given in *Economic Report of the President*, January, Table D–51, p. 214.

*The Shifting of the Corporation Income Tax*

Table A–2. A

| Year | Total capital base | | | Equity base | | |
|------|---------|---------|---------|---------|---------|---------|
| | $Y_{g,t}$ [a] | $Z_t^*$ [b] | $L_t$ [c] | $Y_{g,t}$ [d] | $Z_t^*$ [e] | $L_t$ [f] |
| 1935 | .049108 | .163594 | .008034 | .048019 | .193777 | .009305 |
| 1936 | .089138 | .149023 | .013284 | .096092 | .162424 | .015608 |
| 1937 | .089987 | .158821 | .014292 | .095381 | .174707 | .016664 |
| 1938 | .039436 | .193548 | .007633 | .038822 | .232355 | .009020 |
| 1939 | .079868 | .161406 | .012891 | .086258 | .176735 | .015245 |
| 1940 | .113422 | .273033 | .030968 | .124938 | .291211 | .036383 |
| 1941 | .206268 | .458611 | .094597 | .233222 | .473883 | .110520 |
| 1942 | .245467 | .584426 | .143458 | .279852 | .602333 | .168564 |
| 1948 | .205231 | .364303 | .074766 | .234509 | .375952 | .088164 |
| 1949 | .148368 | .368197 | .054629 | .168334 | .384768 | .064769 |
| 1950 | .232355 | .436514 | .101426 | .265557 | .448017 | .118974 |
| 1951 | .223734 | .551762 | .123448 | .254459 | .569392 | .144887 |
| 1952 | .167488 | .534930 | .089594 | .193106 | .561143 | .108360 |
| 1953 | .165112 | .539015 | .088998 | .194372 | .566368 | .110086 |
| 1954 | .136950 | .487128 | .066712 | .159771 | .516113 | .082460 |
| 1955 | .183334 | .478825 | .087681 | .216362 | .499612 | .108097 |
| 1956 | .161384 | .472210 | .076207 | .186941 | .498571 | .093204 |
| 1957 | .139724 | .472800 | .066061 | .162985 | .506820 | .082604 |
| 1958 | .109546 | .465337 | .050976 | .125790 | .509620 | .064105 |
| 1959 | .138717 | .460942 | .063941 | .117530 | .497678 | .082906 |

[a] Equals col. (2) + (4) : (5) + (6) from Table A–1.
[b] Equals col. (3) : (2) + (4) from Table A–1.
[c] Equals col. (3) : (5) + (6) from Table A–1.
[d] Equals col. (2) : (5) from Table A–1.

Manufacturing, Variables

| Equity base, corrected for inflation[g] | | | Variables common to all cases | | | |
|---|---|---|---|---|---|---|
| $Y_{g,t}$ | $Z_t^*$ | $L_t$ | $\Delta C_{t-1}$ | $V_{t-1}$ | $J_t$ | $G_t$ |
| .044526 | .222123 | .009890 | −.032633 | .246 | .120493 | .163241 |
| .091675 | .177751 | .016295 | −.024982 | .211 | .105749 | .167095 |
| .098975 | .174785 | .017299 | −.025662 | .200 | .134303 | .153320 |
| .051861 | .171615 | .008900 | −.011758 | .220 | .137539 | .178791 |
| .075031 | .199657 | .014981 | .021508 | .246 | .127175 | .172577 |
| .120290 | .299184 | .035990 | −.018080 | .211 | .123457 | .163984 |
| .193174 | .561224 | .108414 | −.021321 | .204 | .119526 | .215540 |
| .245698 | .655460 | .161045 | −.057149 | .195 | .118894 | .398553 |
| .175759 | .443369 | .077926 | .012028 | .170 | .142191 | .155230 |
| .146839 | .386916 | .056815 | −.012715 | .168 | .135704 | .173979 |
| .192321 | .554934 | .106726 | .016158 | .164 | .133145 | .153285 |
| .212741 | .623265 | .132594 | −.014727 | .165 | .159027 | .198961 |
| .165907 | .587087 | .097402 | −.044312 | .178 | .173070 | .235840 |
| .157078 | .637389 | .100120 | −.006257 | .178 | .171414 | .244546 |
| .131140 | .578809 | .075905 | .001677 | .171 | .161355 | .222847 |
| .178057 | .568377 | .101203 | .020446 | .171 | .162317 | .200680 |
| .150268 | .583880 | .087738 | −.002486 | .161 | .171631 | .194056 |
| .128753 | .594058 | .076487 | .006880 | .174 | .168377 | .198082 |
| .099020 | .594574 | .058875 | .004414 | .170 | .164791 | .211547 |
| .128005 | .438034 | .056070 | .020906 | .210 | .169882 | .202813 |

als col. (3) : (2) from Table A–1.
als col. (3) : (5) from Table A–1.
underlying correction procedure see p. 76.

# B

# ADJUSTMENT FOR CHANGES IN PRICE LEVEL

In the income statement and balance sheet data most of the items are recorded in terms of current dollars, but some, including depreciable assets, are recorded in terms of historical cost. The question arises whether and how to reflate such data to make them comparable over time. This adjustment is applied to the case of all manufacturing only.

The appropriate procedure of reflation is determined to some degree by the purpose at hand. The usual purpose is to obtain a "true" picture of the financial accounts, undistorted by price changes. Adjustment for price change may be needed to study changes in wage-profit shares, to examine the growth of productive capacity, or to redefine taxable income in real terms. Our purpose differs. It is to explore whether the determination of the rate of return, and especially the role of tax rates therein, may be carried out better with the use of the adjusted or the unadjusted data. There is no initial presumption that the use of the adjusted data is to be preferred, such as may be the case for certain other purposes. Rather, our final choice depends on the results of the estimates. As noted in the text, these turned out to be slightly in favor of the unadjusted data.

To correct for inflation, we adjust profits to exclude those due to inventory valuation. Also, we must adjust the book value of net fixed capital, consisting of depreciable assets, depletable assets, and land. These must be expressed in the current dollars in which profits or sales or debts are expressed. The resulting increase or decrease in the value of net fixed capital then requires a corresponding increase or reduction in the value of equity. Once the capital value is reflated from historical cost to replacement cost in current dollars, certain other items in the firm's income statement must be adjusted as well to maintain the overall balance of the accounts.

Ideally, the various components of fixed capital, including depreciable assets, depletable assets, and land, require separate reflators, corresponding to their particular replacement costs. Instead, they were lumped together

76

and a common reflator was applied. This simplifies matters and will not result in serious error since depreciable assets are much the most important part of total fixed capital.[1] Thus a common reflator was derived and applied to combined net fixed assets.

## Price Index for Fixed Capital

To reflate "capital" we start from an index of prices of investment goods.[2] In deflating GNP, the Department of Commerce gives price deflators for (1) new construction other than residential non-farm, and (2) producer's durable equipment. (See *Economic Report to the President*, January, 1960). Both series are highly correlated, so that we do not commit a large error by using the average of these two indices as our price index $f_t$. These series begin with 1929, so that a backward extension is needed for our adjustment. For this purpose we use the price index of capital goods, given by Solomon Fabricant, *Capital Consumption and Adjustments* (New York: National Bureau of Economic Research, 1938), Table 32. This index, if multiplied by .47, joins in numerical value our $f_t$ index for 1929 and its extension up to 1935 differs only slightly from $f_t$.

## Age of Capital

The $f_t$ index alone is of little help. "Capital" is a conglomerate of individual items bought at various times in the past and not yet depreciated fully. Thus the age composition of the assets must be considered. S. Fabricant, in his study in *Capital Consumption and Adjustments*, arrives at a time distribution of depreciable goods with an average age of about 20 years. This estimate applies to the years prior to 1935, and there is reason to expect that the consumption of capital goods was accelerated somewhat in later years. Hence a 15-year average recoupment period will be closer to a "true" average for the years since 1936, and is used in our reflation method.

[1] Land usually represents less than 10 per cent of net fixed assets of a firm, and depletable assets are a minor item for manufacturing industries or the firms in our samples.

[2] A series for deflated capital values for all manufacturing is available in Dept. of Commerce, *U.S. Income and Output*, 1958. This series, however, does not extend beyond 1957. Moreover, it seemed desirable to make explicit the underlying assumption regarding the structure of capital. For these and other reasons our independent series was derived. After adjustment for scale (the Dept. of Commerce series relates to all manufacturing, and not to corporations only), the correlation of our and the Dept. of Commerce series over the period of coverage is .99.

*Growth of Capital*

The average recoupment period of 15 years is to be applied to some series of gross investment. For this purpose we consider a hypothetical company that grew at the same pace as investment in non-farm producers' plant and equipment for the U.S. as a whole.[3] For the years from 1929 on, this data is given by the Department of Commerce. (See *Economic Report of the President*, June, 1960.) For the preceding years, we may use a series prepared by Kuznets and Fabricant, (see Carl Shoup, *Principles of National Income Analysis*, Boston, Houghton Mifflin Co., 1947, Table 25, p. 175.) The Kuznets-Fabricant series for private non-residential construction and producers' durable equipment in billions of current dollars if multiplied by .812 joins our series $I_t$ for 1929 and differs only slightly for the overlapping years 1930–38. Unfortunately, this series goes only back to 1919, while data from 1913 on is needed to deflate our series beginning in 1927. For the period 1915–18 we use the value of private and public construction obtained from *Historical Statistics of the U.S.*, series N 1–28. Multiplied by the factor 6.155, this joins the preceding series in 1919. An even cruder method was used to ascertain the $I_t$ series for 1913 and 1914. Because of the small weight of these very early years in our estimates, this should not nullify the usefulness of our reflators for the years 1927–29 and will not affect the estimates from 1933 on.

*Estimation of Reflators*

In estimating the reflators we assume that an imaginary company, beginning with 1913, invested an amount equal to our $I_t$ series. Investments are depreciated on a straight line basis over 15 years. By 1927 only 1/15 of the initial capital is as yet undepreciated. Gross capital in any one year equals the sum of investments over the past 14 and the current year. Depreciation equals 1/15 of this total. The amortization fund equals the sum of depreciation over the past 14 years and the current year. Total fixed assets equal gross fixed assets minus depreciation. All these magnitudes are in historical costs.

To adjust for price change, we translate for each year the historical value of gross investment over the past 14 years into current dollars, i.e., into what these investments would have been had this year's prices prevailed. On the basis of these gross investment figures, we recompute the corresponding depreciation changes. From this, the new figure for the amortization fund is arrived at. Deducting the latter from the gross capital we obtain the revised

[3] The scale of the investment series is of no importance because it cancels out in our formula for reflating indices.

values of net fixed capital. Each series is now in current prices, pertaining to any one year.

The ratio of the current dollar series to the historic cost series are our reflators, including

$r_t$   reflator of depreciation and of gross fixed assets,
$s_t$   reflator of net fixed assets, and
$l_t$   reflator of amortization fund.

As these reflators are applications of averages for the whole economy to industry or individual firm data, the application of all three may lead to discrepancies in accounts. This difficulty is avoided by omitting the $l_t$ reflator, arguing that the sum of net fixed assets and amortization fund must equal gross fixed assets whether in reflated or unreflated values.

To derive the proper formulae for these reflators, let us write:

$D_t$   depreciation of the hypothetical company,
$H_t$   its net fixed assets, and
$K_t$   its gross fixed assets.

If primed, the terms refer to the reflated series, if unprimed, to series without reflation. In terms of our assumptions we define:

$$D_t = \frac{1}{15} \sum_{s=0}^{14} I_{(t-s)} \qquad\qquad D'_t = \frac{f_t}{15} \sum_{s=0}^{14} \frac{I_{t-s}}{f_{(t-s)}}$$

$$K_t = \sum_{s=0}^{14} I_{(t-s)} \qquad\qquad K'_t = f_t \sum_{s=0}^{14} \frac{I_{(t-s)}}{f_{(t-s)}}$$

$$H_t = \frac{1}{15} \sum_{s=0}^{13} I_{(t-s)}(14 - s) \qquad H'_t = \frac{f_t}{15} \sum_{s=0}^{13} \frac{I_{(t-s)}}{f_{(t-s)}}(14 - s)$$

finally,

$$r_t = \frac{D'_t}{D_t} = \frac{K'_t}{K_t} \qquad \text{and} \qquad s_t = \frac{H'_t}{H_t}.$$

*Corrections of Accounts*

The values of $f_t$, $I_t$, $r_t$, and $s_t$ are given in Table B–1. If any industry or firm deducts depreciation $d_t$ from its earnings and the corrected depreciation is noted $d'_t$, then using our reflators

$$d'_t = d_t \cdot r_t.$$

Table B–1.  Price and Investment Indices and Reflators

| Year | $f_t$ | $I_t$ | $r_t$ | $s_t$ |
|------|-------|-------|-------|-------|
| 1913 | .262 | 2.742 | | |
| 4 | .248 | 2.842 | | |
| 5 | .258 | 2.342 | | |
| 6 | .313 | 4.407 | | |
| 7 | .402 | 4.924 | | |
| 8 | .477 | 4.499 | | |
| 9 | .519 | 6.666 | | |
| 1920 | .612 | 7.39 | | |
| 1 | .481 | 5.03 | | |
| 2 | .437 | 5.2 | | |
| 3 | .486 | 7.15 | | |
| 4 | .477 | 6.9 | | |
| 5 | .468 | 7.63 | | |
| 6 | .467 | 8.44 | | |
| 7 | .466 | 8.12 | 1.07826 | .99355 |
| 8 | .461 | 8.36 | 1.03936 | .97893 |
| 9 | .470 | 9.5 | 1.02919 | .99457 |
| 1930 | .451 | 7.4 | .97096 | .95861 |
| 1 | .420 | 4.5 | .88950 | .90267 |
| 2 | .386 | 2.5 | .81501 | .84081 |
| 3 | .375 | 2.3 | .79698 | .82982 |
| 4 | .396 | 3.0 | .85230 | .88957 |
| 5 | .405 | 3.8 | .89437 | .92154 |
| 6 | .403 | 5.1 | .89911 | .93168 |
| 7 | .443 | 6.6 | .98775 | 1.02586 |
| 8 | .446 | 4.7 | 1.00091 | 1.03378 |
| 9 | .439 | 5.3 | .99123 | 1.02012 |
| 1940 | .448 | 7.0 | 1.01540 | 1.03635 |
| 1 | .481 | 8.7 | 1.08701 | 1.09138 |
| 2 | .530 | 5.3 | 1.19111 | 1.17648 |
| 3 | .562 | 4.6 | 1.25254 | 1.21681 |
| 4 | .578 | 6.3 | 1.27184 | 1.20828 |
| 5 | .584 | 9.3 | 1.25057 | 1.16960 |
| 6 | .646 | 14.8 | 1.31200 | 1.20807 |
| 7 | .758 | 20.7 | 1.42572 | 1.28474 |
| 8 | .831 | 23.3 | 1.44925 | 1.28555 |
| 9 | .848 | 21.0 | 1.39668 | 1.23122 |
| 1950 | .870 | 23.4 | 1.35557 | 1.19400 |
| 1 | .949 | 27.4 | 1.38533 | 1.22381 |
| 2 | .970 | 28.1 | 1.33597 | 1.18883 |
| 3 | .989 | 30.2 | 1.29860 | 1.15941 |
| 4 | 1.000 | 29.5 | 1.25777 | 1.13115 |
| 5 | 1.029 | 33.4 | 1.23534 | 1.12462 |
| 6 | 1.099 | 39.4 | 1.25313 | 1.15415 |
| 7 | 1.156 | 41.5 | 1.26775 | 1.16572 |
| 8 | 1.177 | 33.8 | 1.25538 | 1.14998 |
| 9* | 1.207 | 36.9 | 1.24946 | 1.14177 |

* Based on preliminary figures.

Similarly noting gross fixed assets $k_t$ we have

$$k'_t = k_t \cdot r_t$$

and denoting the net fixed assets $h_t$

$$h'_t = h_t \cdot s_t.$$

The correction in firm depreciation must also be applied to profits. The adjusted profits $\pi'$ are:

$$\pi'_t = \pi_t + d_t - d'_t = \pi_t - d_t(r_t - 1).$$

Finally the profit series for manufacturing has to be corrected by adding to it (with proper sign) the inventory valuation adjustment obtained from *U.S. Income and Output*, 1958, Table V–8, for the years from 1940 to 1957. For the years prior to 1940 and for 1958 the series of corporate inventory valuation adjustments, as given in Table I–17 *U.S. Income and Output*, was multiplied by factor .5897 which represents an average correction to change the adjustments for all corporate series into one for manufacturing only.

The correction in the net fixed assets $h_t$ is applied also to the capital figures $c_t$. The adjusted capital $c'_t$ is:

$$c'_t = c_t - h_t + h'_t = c_t + h_t(s_t - 1).$$

# C

# SHIFTING MEASURES

## A. RATE-OF-RETURN INDICATOR

In Chapter 5, two formulations of the shifting measure were proposed, and the first formulation was used thereafter. Both measures were stated in terms of the gross rate of return, in line with the formulation of the dependent variables in our models. Each measure may also be written in net terms without changing its content. We then have these four expressions:

|  | First Formulation | Second Formulation |
|---|---|---|

Gross terms
$$S_{g,t} = \frac{Y_{g,t} - Y_t'}{Z_t^* Y_{g,t}} \qquad S_{g,t}^* = \frac{(1 - Z_t^*)Y_{g,t} - (1 - Z_t^*)Y}{Z_t^* Y_t'}$$

Net terms
$$S_{n,t} = \frac{Y_{n,t} - (1 - Z_t^*)Y_t'}{Z_t^* Y_{n,t}} \qquad S_{n,t}^* = \frac{Y_{n,t} - (1 - Z_t^*)Y_t'}{Z_t^* Y_t'}$$

From the net formulae it is immediately seen that $S_{n,t} > S_{n,t}^*$ for shifting less than 100 per cent, since the measures differ only in the denominator, and $Y_{n,t} < Y_t'$.[1] For shifting in excess of 100 per cent, $S_{n,t} < S_{n,t}^*$, since $Y_{n,t} > Y_t'$. For zero and 100 per cent shifting, $S_{n,t} = S_{n,t}^*$. The same holds for the gross formulations as they are interchangeable with their respective net terms. For example,

$$S_g > S_g^* \text{ for } 0 < S_g < 100\%, \text{ and } S_g < S_g^* \text{ for } S_g > 100\%.$$

[1] For shifting less than zero per cent, the coefficients are negative and the same holds in absolute values.

83

Table C–1. Summary of Shifting Measures in Both Models
(Unlagged Tax Variable)

| Measure | Model A[a] | Model B[b] |
|---|---|---|
| $S_{g,t}$ | $a_4$ | $\dfrac{b_4}{Y_{g,t}}$ |
| $S_{n,t}$ | $1 + A_4 = a_4$ | $1 + \dfrac{(1 - Z_t^*)B_4}{Y_{n,t}}$ |
| $S_g^*$ | $\dfrac{(1 - Z_t^*)a_4}{1 - a_4 Z_t^*}$ | $\dfrac{(1 - Z_t^*)\dfrac{b_4}{Y_{g,t}}}{1 - Z_t^* \dfrac{b_4}{Y_{g,t}}}$ |
| $S_n^*$ | $1 + \dfrac{A_4}{1 - (A_4 + 1)Z_t^*}$ | $1 + \dfrac{\dfrac{B_4}{Y_{n,t}}}{1 - Z_t^* \dfrac{B_4}{Y_{n,t}}}$ |

[a] The gross and net rate models under the same concept of shifting yield identical measurements as the models are comparable and $A_4 + 1 = a_4$.
[b] The gross and net rate models are not consistent in Model **B**.

Table C–2. Summary of Shifting Measures
(Total Effect Over time)

| Measure | Model A[a] | Model B[b] |
|---|---|---|
| $S_{g,t}$ | $\left(a_4 + a_6 \dfrac{L_{t-1}}{L_t}\right)$ | $\left(\dfrac{b_4}{Y_{g,t}} + \dfrac{b_6}{Y_{g,t}} \dfrac{Z_{t-1}^*}{Z_t^*}\right)$ |
| $S_{n,t}$ | $\left(1 + A_4 + A_6 \dfrac{L_{t-1}}{L_t}\right)$ | $1 + (1 - Z_t^*)\left(\dfrac{B_4}{Y_{n,t}} + \dfrac{B_6}{Y_{n,t}} \dfrac{Z_{t-1}^*}{Z_t^*}\right)$ |
| $S_g^*$ | $\dfrac{(1 - Z_t^*)a_4 + a_6 \dfrac{L_{t-1}}{L_t}}{1 - Z_t^*\left(a_4 + a_6 \dfrac{L_{t-1}}{L_t}\right)}$ | $\dfrac{(1 - Z_t^*)\left(\dfrac{b_4}{Y_{g,t}} + \dfrac{b_6}{Y_{g,t}} \dfrac{Z_{t-1}^*}{Z_t^*}\right)}{1 - Z_t^*\left(\dfrac{b_4}{Y_{g,t}} + \dfrac{b_6}{Y_{g,t}} \dfrac{Z_{t-1}^*}{Z_t^*}\right)}$ |
| $S_{n,t}^*$ | $1 + \dfrac{\left(A_4 + A_6 \dfrac{L_{t-1}}{L_t}\right)}{1 - \left(A_4 + 1 + A_6 \dfrac{L_{t-1}}{L_t}\right)Z_t^*}$ | $1 + \dfrac{\dfrac{B_4}{Y_{n,t}} + \dfrac{B_6}{Y_{n,t}} \dfrac{Z_{t-1}^*}{Z_t^*}}{1 - Z_t^*\left(\dfrac{B_4}{Y_{n,t}} + \dfrac{B_6}{Y_{n,t}} \dfrac{Z_{t-1}^*}{Z_t^*}\right)}$ |

[a] The gross and net rate models under the same concept of shifting yield identical measurements as the models are comparable and $A_4 + 1 = a_4$.
[b] The gross and net rate models are not consistent in Model **B**.

## Model A

These observations hold for Model A and B alike, but additional differences arise when introducing the formulations into the different models. We begin with Model A.

*Comparison of $S_{g,t}$ with $S^*_{g,t}$.* In the text, we have used the $S_{g,t}$ measure of shifting for Model A. We now apply the $S^*_{g,t}$ measure in the same way. The two measures are shown in Table C–1 for the unlagged tax variable and in Table C–2 for the combined variables

For the unlagged variable, the $S$ measure is equal to the value of the regression coefficient, thus being independent of the levels of tax rate and rate of return. This is not the case for the $S^*_{g,t}$ measure, the value of which depends on the tax rate. The values of $S_{g,t}$ and $S^*_{g,t}$ for various levels of $a_4$ and $Z^*$ are given in Chart C–1 and in Tables C–3 and C–4. As shown most clearly by the chart, $S_{g,t}$ and the tax regression coefficient coincide for the unlagged tax variable. The value of $S^*_{g,t}$ rises at an increasing rate with the regression coefficient and (for coefficients between zero and 100 per cent) is related inversely to the tax rate.

Chart C–1

Shifting Measures for Model A

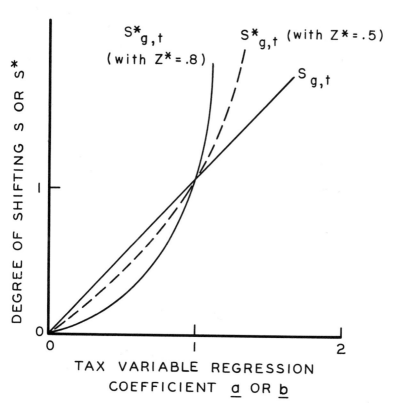

Since a lagged tax variable is also included in the model, these relations are somewhat blurred for the combined measure of shifting, since the coefficient of the lagged tax variable gives a meaning of shifting which depends on the change in tax rate over time.

Table C–3.  Shifting Measures $S_{g,t}$ and $S_{n,t}$ as a Function of the Coefficient

| $Z_t^*$ | $a_4$ or $(A_4 + 1)$ or $\dfrac{b_4}{Y_{g,t}}$ —2.0 | —1.5 | —1.0 | —.9 | —.8 | —.7 | —.6 | —.5 | —.4 |
|---|---|---|---|---|---|---|---|---|---|
| 0 | —2.0 | —1.5 | —1.0 | —.9 | —.8 | —.7 | —.6 | —.5 | —.4 |
| .1 | —2.0 | —1.5 | —1.0 | —.9 | —.8 | —.7 | —.6 | —.5 | —.4 |
| .2 | —2.0 | —1.5 | —1.0 | —.9 | —.8 | —.7 | —.6 | —.5 | —.4 |
| .3 | —2.0 | —1.5 | —1.0 | —.9 | —.8 | —.7 | —.6 | —.5 | —.4 |
| .4 | —2.0 | —1.5 | —1.0 | —.9 | —.8 | —.7 | —.6 | —.5 | —.4 |
| .5 | —2.0 | —1.5 | —1.0 | —.9 | —.8 | —.7 | —.6 | —.5 | —.4 |
| .6 | —2.0 | —1.5 | —1.0 | —.9 | —.8 | —.7 | —.6 | —.5 | —.4 |
| .7 | —2.0 | —1.5 | —1.0 | —.9 | —.8 | —.7 | —.6 | —.5 | —.4 |
| .8 | —2.0 | —1.5 | —1.0 | —.9 | —.8 | —.7 | —.6 | —.5 | —.4 |
| .9 | —2.0 | —1.5 | —1.0 | —.9 | —.8 | —.7 | —.6 | —.5 | —.4 |
| 1.0 | —2.0 | —1.5 | —1.0 | —.9 | —.8 | —.7 | —.6 | —.5 | —.4 |

Table C–4.  Shifting Measures $S_{g,t}^*$ and $S_{n,t}^*$ as a Function of the Coefficient

| $Z_t^*$ | $a_4$ or $(A_4 + 1)$ or $\dfrac{b_4}{Y_{g,t}}$ —2.0 | —1.5 | —1.0 | —.9 | —.8 | —.7 | —.6 | —.5 | —.4 | —.3 |
|---|---|---|---|---|---|---|---|---|---|---|
| 0 | —2.0 | —1.50 | —1.00 | —.90 | —.80 | —.70 | —.60 | —.50 | —.40 | —.30 |
| .1 | —1.50 | —1.17 | —.82 | —.74 | —.67 | —.59 | —.51 | —.43 | —.35 | —.26 |
| .2 | —1.14 | —.92 | —.67 | —.61 | —.55 | —.49 | —.43 | —.36 | —.30 | —.23 |
| .3 | —.88 | —.72 | —.54 | —.50 | —.45 | —.40 | —.36 | —.30 | —.25 | —.19 |
| .4 | —.67 | —.56 | —.43 | —.40 | —.36 | —.33 | —.29 | —.25 | —.21 | —.16 |
| .5 | —.50 | —.43 | —.33 | —.31 | —.29 | —.26 | —.23 | —.20 | —.17 | —.13 |
| .6 | —.36 | —.32 | —.25 | —.23 | —.22 | —.20 | —.18 | —.15 | —.13 | —.10 |
| .7 | —.25 | —.22 | —.18 | —.17 | —.15 | —.14 | —.13 | —.11 | —.09 | —.07 |
| .8 | —.15 | —.14 | —.11 | —.10 | —.10 | —.08 | —.08 | —.07 | —.06 | —.05 |
| .9 | —.07 | —.06 | —.05 | —.05 | —.05 | —.04 | —.04 | —.03 | —.03 | —.02 |
| 1.0 | 0 | 0 | 0 | 0 | 0 | 0 | 0 | 0 | 0 | 0 |

It remains to compare the specific results obtained in the text by the use of $S_{g,t}$ with those which would have been obtained had $S^*_{g,t}$ been used. This is shown in Table C–5 for the all-manufacturing case. Shifting for $S_{g,t}$, the unlagged tax variable, Model A, was 134 per cent for $S_{g,t}$ and 171 per cent for

for Unlagged Tax Variable and Effective Tax Rate (Model A and Model B Gross.)

| −.3 | −.2 | −.1 | 0 | .1 | .2 | .3 | .4 | .5 | .6 | .7 | .8 | .9 | 1.0 | 1.5 | 2.0 |
|---|---|---|---|---|---|---|---|---|---|---|---|---|---|---|---|
| −.3 | −.2 | −.1 | 0 | .1 | .2 | .3 | .4 | .5 | .6 | .7 | .8 | .9 | 1.0 | 1.5 | 2.0 |
| −.3 | −.2 | −.1 | 0 | .1 | .2 | .3 | .4 | .5 | .6 | .7 | .8 | .9 | 1.0 | 1.5 | 2.0 |
| −.3 | −.2 | −.1 | 0 | .1 | .2 | .3 | .4 | .5 | .6 | .7 | .8 | .9 | 1.0 | 1.5 | 2.0 |
| −.3 | −.2 | −.1 | 0 | .1 | .2 | .3 | .4 | .5 | .6 | .7 | .8 | .9 | 1.0 | 1.5 | 2.0 |
| −.3 | −.2 | −.1 | 0 | .1 | .2 | .3 | .4 | .5 | .6 | .7 | .8 | .9 | 1.0 | 1.5 | 2.0 |
| −.3 | −.2 | −.1 | 0 | .1 | .2 | .3 | .4 | .5 | .6 | .7 | .8 | .9 | 1.0 | 1.5 | 2.0 |
| −.3 | −.2 | −.1 | 0 | .1 | .2 | .3 | .4 | .5 | .6 | .7 | .8 | .9 | 1.0 | 1.5 | 2.0 |
| −.3 | −.2 | −.1 | 0 | .1 | .2 | .3 | .4 | .5 | .6 | .7 | .8 | .9 | 1.0 | 1.5 | 2.0 |
| −.3 | −.2 | −.1 | 0 | .1 | .2 | .3 | .4 | .5 | .6 | .7 | .8 | .9 | 1.0 | 1.5 | 2.0 |
| −.3 | −.2 | −.1 | 0 | .1 | .2 | .3 | .4 | .5 | .6 | .7 | .8 | .9 | 1.0 | 1.5 | 2.0 |
| −.3 | −.2 | −.1 | 0 | .1 | .2 | .3 | .4 | .5 | .6 | .7 | .8 | .9 | 1.0 | 1.5 | 2.0 |

for Unlagged Tax Variable and Effective Tax Rate (Model A and Model B Gross.)

| −.2 | −.1 | 0 | .1 | .2 | .3 | .4 | .5 | .6 | .7 | .8 | .9 | 1.0 | 1.5 | 2.0 |
|---|---|---|---|---|---|---|---|---|---|---|---|---|---|---|
| −.20 | −.1 | 0 | .10 | .20 | .30 | .40 | .50 | .60 | .70 | .80 | .90 | 1.00 | 1.50 | 2.00 |
| −.18 | −.09 | 0 | .09 | .18 | .28 | .38 | .47 | .57 | .68 | .78 | .89 | 1.00 | 1.59 | 2.25 |
| −.15 | −.08 | 0 | .08 | .17 | .26 | .35 | .44 | .55 | .65 | .76 | .88 | 1.00 | 1.71 | 2.67 |
| −.13 | −.07 | 0 | .07 | .15 | .23 | .32 | .41 | .51 | .62 | .74 | .86 | 1.00 | 1.91 | 3.50 |
| −.11 | −.06 | 0 | .06 | .13 | .20 | .29 | .38 | .47 | .58 | .71 | .84 | 1.00 | 2.25 | 6.00 |
| −.09 | −.05 | 0 | .05 | .11 | .18 | .25 | .33 | .43 | .54 | .67 | .82 | 1.00 | 3.00 | $+\infty$ |
|  |  |  |  |  |  |  |  |  |  |  |  |  |  | $-\infty$ |
| −.07 | −.04 | 0 | .04 | .09 | .15 | .21 | .29 | .38 | .48 | .62 | .78 | 1.00 | 6.00 | −4.00 |
| −.05 | −.03 | 0 | .03 | .07 | .11 | .17 | .23 | .31 | .41 | .55 | .73 | 1.00 | −9.00 | −1.50 |
| −.03 | −.02 | 0 | .02 | .05 | .08 | .12 | .17 | .23 | .32 | .44 | .64 | 1.00 | −1.50 | −.67 |
| −.02 | −.01 | 0 | .01 | .02 | .04 | .06 | .09 | .13 | .19 | .29 | .47 | 1.00 | −.43 | −.25 |
| 0 | 0 | 0 | 0 | 0 | 0 | 0 | 0 | 0 | 0 | 0 | 0 | ? | 0 | 0 |

$S_{g,t}^*$, thus indicating that the same coefficients obtained from the same model suggest quite different degrees of shifting, depending on the concept used.

Table C–5.  Degrees of Shifting Under Different Measures,
Estimated for All Manufacturing, Total Capital Base

|  | Model A | Model B |
|---|---|---|
| Description | For unlagged tax variable | For unlagged tax variable |
| First concept: | | |
| $S_g$. | 1.3394 | 1.8836 |
| $S_n$. | 1.3394 | 1.8012[a] |
| Second concept: | | |
| $S_g^*$. | 1.7080 | 4.2988 |
| $S_n^*$. | 1.7080 | 3.6926[a] |

[a] As noted on page 26 *note 8*. The net rate of return, Model B measures are not consistent with those of gross rate measures.

*Comparison of Net and Gross Formulations.*  So far the discussion has been in terms of gross rates of return and the corresponding shifting concepts.  If the rate-of-return function is written in net terms, the function remains consistent for model A with the gross formulation.  All coefficients are the same for both functions, except for the unlagged tax variable.  Using capital letters for the coefficients of the net rate function we have $A_4 = a_4 - 1$.  This is the case because $Y_{g,t} - L_t = Y_{n,t}$.

Since the rate-of-return functions are consistent in gross and net terms, application of the respective gross and net measures also leaves us with the same results.  This is shown in Tables C–1, C–2 and C–5.  This is one of the advantages of model A over model B, where the results for the gross and net formulations differ.

## Model B

*Comparison of $S_{g,t}$ and $S_{g,t}^*$.*  The comparison between the two measures in gross terms is given in Tables C–1 and C–2.  For the unlagged tax variable, $S_{g,t}$ depends not only on the coefficient, but also inversely on the rate of return and, through the latter, on the tax rate.  The relationship is much more complex than that for model A and cannot be summarized in simple tables corresponding to C–3 and C–4.  However, these tables may be interpreted as giving a partial view of the relation for model B.  Table C–3 may be taken to record the values of $S_{g,t}$ for model B, if the values in the horizontal scale are read to equal $\dfrac{b_4}{Y_{g,t}}$. Table C–4, similarly, may be taken to record the values of $S^*_{g,t}$ for model B, if the horizontal scale is taken to measure $\dfrac{b_4}{Y_{g,t}}$.

*Comparison of Net and Gross Formulations.* Whereas the results for the gross and net approaches are similar in model A, they differ for model B. This is the case because the rate of return function for model B, if linear in gross terms, cannot be linear in net terms and vice versa.

Comparing $S_{g,t}$ with $S_{n,t}$ as shown in Table C–1, we note that the shifting measures differ, and in a complicated fashion. A partial view may be obtained from Table C–6 for the behavior of $S_{n,t}$, assuming given values of $\dfrac{B_4}{Y_{n,t}}$. The same view is given for $S^*_{n,t}$ in Table C–7. Both shifting patterns are difficult to interpret.

*Comparison of Results for All-Manufacturing.* Table C–5 also shows the degrees of shifting for the all-manufacturing, total capital base case, assuming the four shifting measures to be used.[2] The results of the two gross measures $S_{g.}$ and $S^*_{g.}$ for model B differ more sharply than for model A and so do $S_{n.}$ and $S^*_{n.}$. Further, the starred measures show extremely high values as well as high standard errors. This is to be expected if one notes the complex behavior of the measure for more than 100 per cent shifting (see Tables C–4 and C–7). The temperamental behavior of the starred shifting concept is an important reason for adopting the unstarred concept in our analysis.

---

[2] The net measures were computed from the following estimate of the net rate of return function:
$$Y_{n,t} = B_0 + .5089\,\Delta C_{t-1} - .5707\,V_{t-1} - 1.1884\,J_t + .1085\,Z_t + U_t; \quad R = .8251$$
$$\quad\quad\quad\; [.8879] \quad\quad\quad [-3.0913] \quad [-5.1987] \quad [2.9875]$$

Table C–6. Partial Shifting Measure $S_{n,t}$ as a Function of the

| $\frac{B_4}{Y_{n,t}}$ <br> $Z_t^*$ | $-3.0$ | $-2.5$ | $-2.0$ | $-1.9$ | $-1.8$ | $-1.7$ | $-1.6$ | $-1.5$ | $-1.4$ | $-1.3$ | $-1.2$ |
|---|---|---|---|---|---|---|---|---|---|---|---|
| 0 | $-2.0$ | $-1.5$ | $-1.0$ | $-.90$ | $-.80$ | $-.70$ | $-.60$ | $-.50$ | $-.40$ | $-.30$ | $-.20$ |
| .1 | $-1.70$ | $-1.25$ | $-.80$ | $-.71$ | $-.62$ | $-.53$ | $-.44$ | $-.35$ | $-.26$ | $-.17$ | $-.08$ |
| .2 | $-1.40$ | $-1.0$ | $-.60$ | $-.52$ | $-.44$ | $-.36$ | $-.28$ | $-.20$ | $-.12$ | $-.04$ | .04 |
| .3 | $-1.10$ | $-.75$ | $-.40$ | $-.33$ | $-.26$ | $-.19$ | $-.12$ | $-.05$ | $-.02$ | .09 | .16 |
| .4 | $-.80$ | $-.50$ | $-.20$ | $-.14$ | $-.08$ | $-.02$ | .04 | .10 | .16 | .22 | .28 |
| .5 | $-.50$ | $-.25$ | 0 | .05 | .10 | .15 | .20 | .25 | .30 | .35 | .40 |
| .6 | $-.20$ | 0 | .20 | .24 | .28 | .32 | .36 | .40 | .44 | .48 | .52 |
| .7 | .10 | .25 | .40 | .43 | .46 | .49 | .52 | .55 | .58 | .61 | .64 |
| .8 | .40 | .50 | .60 | .62 | .64 | .66 | .68 | .70 | .72 | .74 | .76 |
| .9 | .70 | .75 | .80 | .81 | .82 | .83 | .84 | .85 | .86 | .87 | .88 |
| 1.0 | 1.00 | 1.00 | 1.00 | 1.00 | 1.00 | 1.00 | 1.00 | 1.00 | 1.00 | 1.00 | 1.00 |

Table C–7. Partial Shifting Measure $S_{n,t}^*$ as a Function of the

| $\frac{B_4}{Y_{n,t}}$ <br> $Z_t^*$ | $-3.0$ | $-2.5$ | $-2.0$ | $-1.9$ | $-1.8$ | $-1.7$ | $-1.6$ | $-1.5$ | $-1.4$ | $-1.3$ | $-1.2$ |
|---|---|---|---|---|---|---|---|---|---|---|---|
| 0 | $-2.0$ | $-1.5$ | $-1.0$ | $-.9$ | $-.8$ | $-.7$ | $-.6$ | $-.5$ | $-.4$ | $-.3$ | $-.2$ |
| .1 | $-1.31$ | $-1.0$ | $-.67$ | $-.60$ | $-.53$ | $-.45$ | $-.38$ | $-.30$ | $-.23$ | $-.15$ | $-.07$ |
| .2 | $-.87$ | $-.67$ | $-.43$ | $-.38$ | $-.32$ | $-.27$ | $-.21$ | $-.15$ | $-.09$ | $-.03$ | .03 |
| .3 | $-.58$ | $-.43$ | $-.25$ | $-.21$ | $-.17$ | $-.13$ | $-.08$ | $-.03$ | .01 | .06 | .12 |
| .4 | $-.36$ | $-.25$ | $-.11$ | $-.08$ | $-.05$ | $-.01$ | .02 | .06 | .10 | .14 | .19 |
| .5 | $-.20$ | $-.11$ | 0 | .03 | .05 | .08 | .11 | .14 | .18 | .21 | .25 |
| .6 | $-.07$ | 0 | .09 | .11 | .13 | .16 | .18 | .21 | .24 | .27 | .30 |
| .7 | .03 | .09 | .17 | .18 | .20 | .22 | .25 | .27 | .29 | .32 | .35 |
| .8 | .12 | .17 | .23 | .25 | .26 | .28 | .30 | .32 | .34 | .36 | .39 |
| .9 | .19 | .23 | .29 | .30 | .31 | .33 | .34 | .36 | .38 | .40 | .42 |
| 1.0 | .25 | .29 | .33 | .34 | .36 | .37 | .38 | .40 | .42 | .43 | .45 |

Coefficient for Unlagged Tax Variable and Effective Tax Rate (Model B)

| −1.1 | −1.0 | −.9 | −.8 | −.7 | −.6 | −.5 | −.4 | −.3 | −.2 | −.1 | 0 | .5 | 1.0 |
|---|---|---|---|---|---|---|---|---|---|---|---|---|---|
| −.10 | 0 | .10 | .20 | .30 | .40 | .50 | .60 | .70 | .80 | .90 | 1.00 | 1.50 | 2.00 |
| .01 | .10 | .19 | .28 | .37 | .46 | .55 | .64 | .73 | .82 | .91 | 1.00 | 1.45 | 1.90 |
| .12 | .20 | .28 | .36 | .44 | .52 | .60 | .68 | .76 | .84 | .92 | 1.00 | 1.40 | 1.80 |
| .23 | .30 | .37 | .44 | .51 | .58 | .65 | .72 | .79 | .86 | .93 | 1.00 | 1.35 | 1.70 |
| .34 | .40 | .46 | .52 | .58 | .64 | .70 | .76 | .82 | .88 | .94 | 1.00 | 1.30 | 1.60 |
| .45 | .50 | .55 | .60 | .65 | .70 | .75 | .80 | .85 | .90 | .95 | 1.00 | 1.25 | 1.50 |
| .56 | .60 | .64 | .68 | .72 | .76 | .80 | .84 | .88 | .92 | .96 | 1.00 | 1.20 | 1.40 |
| .67 | .70 | .73 | .76 | .79 | .82 | .85 | .88 | .91 | .94 | .97 | 1.00 | 1.15 | 1.30 |
| .78 | .80 | .82 | .84 | .86 | .88 | .90 | .92 | .94 | .96 | .98 | 1.00 | 1.10 | 1.20 |
| .89 | .90 | .91 | .92 | .93 | .94 | .95 | .96 | .97 | .98 | .99 | 1.00 | 1.05 | 1.10 |
| 1.00 | 1.00 | 1.00 | 1.00 | 1.00 | 1.00 | 1.00 | 1.00 | 1.00 | 1.00 | 1.00 | 1.00 | 1.00 | 1.00 |

Coefficient for Unlagged Tax Variable and Effective Tax Rate (Model B)

| −1.1 | −1.0 | −.9 | −.8 | −.7 | −.6 | −.5 | −.4 | −.3 | −.2 | −.1 | 0 | .5 | 1.0 |
|---|---|---|---|---|---|---|---|---|---|---|---|---|---|
| −.1 | 0 | .10 | .20 | .30 | .40 | .50 | .60 | .70 | .80 | .90 | 1 | 1.5 | 2.0 |
| −.01 | −.09 | .17 | .26 | .35 | .43 | .52 | .62 | .71 | .80 | .90 | 1 | 1.53 | 2.01 |
| .10 | .17 | .24 | .31 | .39 | .46 | .55 | .63 | .72 | .81 | .90 | 1 | 1.56 | 2.02 |
| .17 | .23 | .29 | .35 | .42 | .49 | .57 | .64 | .72 | .81 | .90 | 1 | 1.59 | 2.03 |
| .24 | .29 | .34 | .39 | .45 | .52 | .58 | .66 | .73 | .81 | .90 | 1 | 1.63 | 2.04 |
| .29 | .33 | .38 | .43 | .48 | .54 | .60 | .67 | .74 | .82 | .90 | 1 | 1.67 | 2.05 |
| .34 | .37 | .42 | .46 | .51 | .56 | .62 | .68 | .75 | .82 | .91 | 1 | 1.71 | 2.06 |
| .38 | .41 | .45 | .49 | .53 | .58 | .63 | .69 | .75 | .82 | .91 | 1 | 1.77 | 2.08 |
| .41 | .44 | .48 | .51 | .55 | .59 | .64 | .70 | .76 | .83 | .91 | 1 | 1.83 | 2.09 |
| .45 | .47 | .50 | .53 | .57 | .61 | .66 | .71 | .76 | .83 | .91 | 1 | 1.91 | 2.10 |
| .48 | .50 | .53 | .56 | .59 | .62 | .67 | .71 | .77 | .83 | .91 | 1 | 2.0 | ∞ |

## B. SHARE INDICATOR

In Chapter 2, the conditions for zero and 100 per cent shifting were defined as follows:

| Indicator | Zero Shifting | L 100% Shifting |
|-----------|---------------|-----------------|
| Net Share | $F_n = (1 - Z)F'$ | $F_n = F'$ |
| Gross Share | $F_g = F'$ | $(1 - Z^*)F_g = F'$ |

The corresponding measure of shifting for the net share approach must be based on the $S^*$ type formulation expressed in net terms. We obtain

$$S_n^* = \frac{F_n - (1 - Z^*)F'}{Z^*F'}.$$

The corresponding measure for the gross share approach must be based on the $S$ type formulation expressed in gross terms, hence we obtain

$$S_g = \frac{F_g - F'}{Z^*F_g}$$

# D

# STANDARD ERROR OF SHIFTING MEASURE

In the tables pertaining to Chapters 6 and 7, we follow the standard procedure of noting below the coefficients in square brackets the value of the $t$ test,

$$t_i = \frac{a_i}{\sigma_{ai}},$$

which measures the significance of the coefficients. Underneath the shifting measures, we enter in round brackets its standard error. The estimation of this error needs brief discussion.

For model A, the estimate of the shifting measure is given by the coefficient of $L_t$ and the standard error of the coefficient is common to both. This is not the case in model B. To obtain the shifting measure, the coefficient is now divided by a constant $Y_g.$ or $S_g. = \dfrac{b_4}{Y_g.}$. Consequently the standard error of the estimate of shifting is

$$\sigma_S. = \frac{\sigma_{b4}}{Y_g.}.$$

In the few cases where the statutory rate is used, the estimate of the measure of shifting is

$$S_g. = b_4 \frac{Z.}{L.}$$

and its standard error is

$$\sigma_S. = \sigma_{b4} \frac{Z.}{L.}.$$

Where the lagged tax variable is used, the shifting measures and their standard errors are computed as follows:

|  | Model A | Model B |
|---|---|---|
| $S_{g.-1}$ | $a_6 \dfrac{L._{-1}}{L.}$ | $b_6 \dfrac{Z^*._{-1}}{L.}$ |
| $\sigma_{S.-1}$ | $\sigma_{a6} \dfrac{L._{-1}}{L.}$ | $\sigma_{b6} \dfrac{Z^*._{-1}}{L.}$ |

To arrive at an estimate of the combined degree of shifting, the measures are added, and the standard error of the combined measure is

$$\sigma_S = \sqrt{\sigma_{S.0}^2 + \sigma_{S.-1}^2 + 2 \operatorname{Cov}_{S.0, S.-1}}$$

The covariance of this measure equals the covariance of the coefficients for the lagged and unlagged tax variables multiplied by their respective weights.

# E

# ASSUMPTIONS, TESTS, AND ESTIMATING PROCEDURES

## A. ASSUMPTIONS UNDERLYING MODEL B.

The model B equation was written as follows:[1]

$$Y_{g,t} = b_0 + b_1 \Delta C_{t-1} + b_2 V_{t-1} + b_3 J_t + b_4 Z_t + U_t$$

and was estimated by least squares method. To have "good" properties, such estimates must come from an equation in which the variables satisfy certain assumptions. In our model B cases, the assumptions are:

1. All variables on the right side of the above noted equation are predetermined, i.e., either exogenous or lagged endogenous. Predetermined variables are not correlated with the stochastic variable $U_t$. If we note the predetermined variables as $Z_{i,t}(i = 1, 2 \ldots n.)$ (This notation will be used only for this appendix.), we have

$$E(U_t Z_{i,t,}) = 0, \ (i = 1, 2 \ldots n.)$$

where notation $E$ stands for statistical term expectation

2. The stochastic variable $U_t$ has the following properties:

$E(U_t) = 0$ for all $t$

$E(U_t^2) = \sigma_u^2$ a finite number and constant in time (homoschedastic)

3. The stochastic variable is not auto-correlated with its preceding values, or

$$E(U_t U_{t-s}) = 0 \text{ for } s \neq 0.$$

4. Specifically, it is assumed that the stochastic variable is normally distributed with mean zero and variance $\sigma_u^2$.

[1] See p. 34 and p. 50, Table 6–3, line 3.

94

5. The predetermined variables are not correlated with each other. If this assumption did not hold, we would have multicollinearity. Two restrictions on our model need to be noted:

    a. Not all predetermined variables are exogenous. In our cases $\Delta C_{t-1}$ and $V_{t-1}$ are lagged endogenous.

    b. The sample size is small; in no case does it exceed 20 observations.

If all 5 assumptions held and all our predetermined variables were exogenous which, as just noted is not the case, our model B estimates would be[2] consistent,[3] unbiased,[4] and efficient.[5] As our model B contains lagged endogenous variables, we may claim that our estimates are: consistent and asymptotically efficient,[6] but they may be biased. If only assumption 4 is invalid, the estimates remain consistent. If only assumption 3 is invalid, the estimates remain consistent,[7] but their errors may be underestimated.[8] If there is multicollinearity, the errors of the collinear variables rise. If our equation lacks homoschedasticity, our estimates become inefficient.[9]

In model B little effort was made to test whether these assumptions in fact hold. Only the auto-correlation in the error term was tested by Durbin-Watson statistics[10] against the hypothesis that

where
$$U_t = BU_{t-1} + E_t,$$
$$E_t \text{ has } [N, O, \sigma_E^2].$$

[2] See Wm. C. Hood and Tjalling C. Koopmans, eds. *Studies in Econometric Method*, Cowles Commission Monograph No. 14 (New York: J. Wiley & Sons, 1953), p. 133.

[3] I.e., the estimates tend to the parameter for the whole population as the sample size rises.

[4] I.e., the expectation of the estimates of a parameter is the parameter for the whole population.

[5] I.e., the error of such estimates is the smallest possible compared with that for any other estimates.

[6] I.e., as the sample size increases without limit, the error of the estimate tends to become the smallest possible, compared with that for any other estimates.

[7] F. N. David and J. Neyman, "Extension of the Markoff Theorem of Least Squares," *Statistical Research Memoirs*, vol. 2, December, 1938, pp. 103–16 prove that serial correlation of the random term in a single equation leaves least squares estimates unbiased and consistent.

[8] *Analytical Tools for Studying Demand and Price Structures*, Agricultural Handbook No. 146 (Washington, D.C.: U.S. Dept. of Agriculture, 1958), p. 161. "The pressure of nonindependent error terms is commonly believed to make the least squares estimate of the variance of the coefficients deceptively small. . . . This may not always be the case."

[9] Stefan Valavanis, *Econometrics* (New York: McGraw-Hill Book Co., 1959), p. 48 states: "Least squares yields . . . inefficient estimates if the variance of $U_t$ is not constant but varies systematically, either with time or with the magnitude of the exogenous variables."

[10] See J. Durbin and G. S. Watson, "Testing for Serial Correlation in Least Squares Regression," *Biometrika*, 37 (1950), pp. 409–28 and *ibid.*, 38 (1951), pp. 159–78. Also see G. S. Watson and E. Brannon, "Serial Correlation in Regression Analysis," *Biometrika*, 43 (1956), pp. 436–48. For results see p. 50, Table 6–3.

Normality was tested for crudely on normal graph paper, and the visual divergence of the observed points from the diagonal was considered small enough to justify the normality assumption. With 20 observation points or less, not much can be done in this respect.

## B. ASSUMPTIONS UNDERLYING MODEL A.

The standard form of this model was written as[11]

$$Y_{g,t} = a_0 + a_1 \Delta C_{t-1} + a_2 V_{t-1} + a_3 J_t + a_4 L_t + U_t$$

The difference from standard model B is that the $L_t$ variable is not a predetermined one. This we see from relation

$$L_t = Z_t^* Y_{g,t}.$$

Obviously $E(L_t U_t) \neq 0$. Even if other variables on the right side satisfy the conditions 1 to 5 of model B, the least squares method would not yield consistent estimates and would be "naïve."

Consequently the instrumental variable approach was chosen to get "better" estimates. Unfortunately, only properties of large sample estimates made under the instrumental variable approach are known exactly, and the samples here studied are all small.

Fortunately not all is lost as there are special circumstances in our case, namely:

1. our equation is clearly identified by the variable $Z_t^*$,
2. only one instrument is needed,
3. collinear variables are removed from the standard model.

Hence the instrumental variable estimates in our study are superior to "naïve" least squares estimates.[12]

The assumptions regarding the stochastic and predetermined variables have to be the same as for model B. The following paragraph examines them.

---

[11] See p. 44, Table 6-1, line 3.

[12] J. D. Sargan, *op. cit.*, p. 412 claims: "Theoretically then, if the asymptotic properties of the two kinds of estimates are compared, the instrumental variables method (provided the relationship is a priori identified) is the better, since the estimates are consistent, whereas the least squares estimates are not. However, for finite $T$, the advantage of using the instrumental variables method is less certain, since the instrumental variables estimates may have large biases especially in the almost unidentified case and in the event the number of instrumental variables is large."

## C. TESTS IN MODEL A.

### a. *Auto-correlation*

Most series were tested for serial auto-correlation, i.e., correlation of the error term with its values in preceding periods. Presence of such correlation may lead to underestimation of the standard error of the regression coefficient and overestimation of $R$.[13] The Durbin-Watson statistic is used for the test.[14] In the test, two special problems arise.

One is that the test is designed for application to error terms computed under the least squares method. Our model A, however, estimates error terms under the instrumental variable approach. In the absence of a more suitable alternative, the test was nevertheless applied.

Another problem is that the test is designed for series which are continuous over time, while our series are broken for the war period. Consequently, differencing of the error terms for 1942 and 1948 had to be omitted in the numerator of the $d$ statistic. For consistency reasons, the error term for the first year following the gap was omitted in the denominator.[15]

### b. *Homoschedasticity*

A basic assumption of our models is that the variance of the prediction error should be constant for the whole range of variation of the predetermined variables and also over time.[16] This property is called homoschedasticity.

In our models, the absolute level of predetermined variables, especially tax variables, was usually low for the prewar period and high for the postwar period. This suggests that the test be based on a comparison of the variances or prediction errors for these two periods. A ratio of such variances is subjected to the $F$ test. The hypothesis is that the variances for the pre- and postwar periods come from the same population, the differences between them arising from random forces.

The following gives the observations for the all-manufacturing, total capital case.[17]

[13] See note 8, p. 95, Appendix E–A.
[14] See note 10, p. 95, Appendix E–A.
[15] This procedure is suggested in *Analytic Tools for Studying Demand and Price Structures, op. cit.*, p. 173.
[16] Valavanis, *Econometrics, op. cit.*, p. 48 states: "Least squares yields . . . inefficient estimates if the variance of $U_t$ is not constant but varies systematically, either with time or with the magnitude of the exogenous variables."
[17] See Table 7–1, Cases No. 2 and 3.

| Description | d.f. | $\sigma_u$ | $F_0 = \dfrac{\sigma_u^2 \text{ prewar}}{\sigma_u^2 \text{ postwar}}$ |
|---|---|---|---|
| Case No. (2), Prewar | 3 | .01563 | 1.12737 |
| Case No. (3), Postwar | 7 | .01472 | |

The observed $F$ ratio of variances may be subjected to the $F$ test given the degrees of freedom and the level of significance required. The observed $F_0$ in the all-manufacturing, total capital base, falls closer to the right hand tail of the $F$ distribution because $\sigma_u^2$ prewar $> \sigma_u^2$ postwar. It is also close to 1, hence, one may accept the hypothesis of homoschedasticity, even at the 70 per cent level of significance. The value of this statistic at that level is $F_c = 1.48$.

## D. ESTIMATING PROCEDURE FOR MODEL A.

A brief outline of the estimating procedures under the instrumental variable approach may be given as follows. The notation used is

$Y_t$—dependent variable, to be explained.

$X_{i,t}$—dependent variables used in explaining $Y_t$.

$Z_{i,t}$—predetermined variables

   $Z_{i,t}^*$ present in the equation

   $Z_{i,t}^{**}$ used as instruments for $X_{i,t}$

      Assume each $X_{i,t}$ has its $Z_{i,t}^{**}$ for its instrument

$U_t$—stochastic variable

$t$—time ($t = 1, 2 \ldots T$).

In this notation the equation to be estimated will be written

$$Y_t = a_0 + \sum_{i=1}^{m} a_i Z_{i,t}^* + \sum_{i=m+1}^{n} a_i X_{i,t} + U_t$$

To compute instrumental variable coefficients we have to compute first variances and covariances and group them in vectors and matrices. Noting them by $M$ as moments we distinguish:

1. Column Vectors of size ($n \times 1$)

$$M_{YZ} = \begin{bmatrix} M_{YZ_1^*} \\ M_{YZ_2^*} \\ \cdots \\ M_{YZ_m^*} \\ M_{YZ_{m+1}^{**}} \\ \cdots \\ M_{YZ_n^{**}} \end{bmatrix} \qquad a = \begin{bmatrix} a_1 \\ a_2 \\ \cdots \\ a_m \\ a_{m+1} \\ \cdots \\ a_n \end{bmatrix}$$

2. Square matrix of size $(m \times m)$

$$M_{Z^*Z^*} = \begin{bmatrix} M_{Z_1^*Z_1^*} & M_{Z_1^*Z_2^*} & \cdots & M_{Z_1^*Z_m^*} \\ M_{Z_2^*Z_1^*} & M_{Z_2^*Z_2^*} & \cdots & M_{Z_2^*Z_m^*} \\ \cdot & \cdot & \cdots & \cdot \\ M_{Z_m^*Z_1^*} & M_{Z_m^*Z_2^*} & \cdots & M_{Z_m^*Z_m^*} \end{bmatrix}$$

3. Square matrix of size $(n - m) \times (n - m)$

$$M_{Z^{**}Z^{**}} = \begin{bmatrix} M_{Z_{m+1}^{**}Z_{m+1}^{**}} & M_{Z_{m+1}^{**}Z_{m+2}^{**}} & M_{Z_{m+1}^{**}Z_n^{**}} \\ M_{Z_{m+2}^{**}Z_{m+1}^{**}} & M_{Z_{m+2}^{**}Z_{m+2}^{**}} & M_{Z_{m+2}^{**}Z_n^{**}} \\ \cdot & \cdot & \cdot \\ M_{Z_n^{**}Z_{m+1}^{**}} & M_{Z_n^{**}Z_{m+2}^{**}} & M_{Z_n^{**}Z_n^{**}} \end{bmatrix}$$

$M_{Z^{**}X}$ is formed analogously

4. Matrix of size $m \times (n - m)$

$$M_{Z^*Z^{**}} = \begin{bmatrix} M_{Z_1^*Z_{m+1}^{**}} & M_{Z_1^*Z_{m+2}^{**}} & \cdots & M_{Z_1^*Z_n^{**}} \\ M_{Z_2^*Z_{m+1}^{**}} & M_{Z_2^*Z_{m+2}^{**}} & \cdots & M_{Z_2^*Z_{m+2}^{**}} \\ \cdot & \cdot & \cdots & \cdot \\ M_{Z_m^*Z_{m+1}^{**}} & M_{Z_m^*Z_{m+2}^{**}} & \cdots & M_{Z_m^*Z_n^{**}} \end{bmatrix}$$

$M_{Z^*X}$ is formed analogously.

Following standard matrix notation, we let prime $A'$ mean a transpose of $A$ and superscript $A^{-1}$ the inverse of $A$.

If we form composite matrix $F$ of size $n \times n$

$$F = \begin{bmatrix} M_{Z^*Z^*} & M_{Z^*X} \\ M'_{Z^*Z^{**}} & M_{Z^{**}X} \end{bmatrix}$$

then the vector of coefficients is computed as follows:

$$a = \begin{bmatrix} a_1 \\ a_2 \\ \cdots \\ a_n \end{bmatrix} = F^{-1}M_{YZ}$$

and

$$a_0 = \frac{1}{T} \left[ \sum_t Y_t - \sum_{i=1}^{m} a_i Z_{i,t}^* - \sum_{i=m+1}^{n} a_i X_{i,t} \right]$$

Next one computes $Y$ predicted for each period. The difference between $Y_t$ observed and $Y_t$ predicted is our estimate of the stochastic variable $U_t$..

Its variance $s_u^2$ yields an estimate of $\sigma_u^2$, which in turn can be used to estimate $R$, the multiple correlation coefficient, adjusted for degrees of freedom.

To estimate the standard errors of the coefficients the matrix $M_{ZZ}$ of size $n \times n$ is formed

$$M_{ZZ} = \begin{bmatrix} M_{Z^*Z^*} & M_{Z^*Z^{**}} \\ M'_{Z^*Z^{**}} & M_{Z^{**}Z^{**}} \end{bmatrix}$$

Followed by formation of a matrix $G$ also of size $n \times n$

$$G = F^{-1}M_{ZZ}F'^{-1}$$

Finally let the square roots of the elements of the trace of this matrix be written as a column vector $K$ of size $n \times 1$, then the column vector of standard error of coefficients $a$ is computed as follows:

$$\sigma_a = \begin{bmatrix} \sigma_{a_1} \\ \sigma_{a_2} \\ \dots \\ \sigma_{a_n} \end{bmatrix} = \sigma_u K \text{ which completes our estimates.}$$

THE SHIFTING OF THE
CORPORATION INCOME TAX

Marian Krzyzaniak and Richard Musgrave

designer: Edward D. King

typesetter: Monotype Composition Co.

typefaces: Text: Times Roman

printer: Universal Lithographers, Inc.

paper: Perkins and Squire, P & S SM

binder: Moore & Company

cover material: Bancroft Arrestox